TORCHBEARERS OF THE TRUTH

"Shining as Lights in the World"

Brief accounts of the lives and labours
of some remarkable servants of God
in the 14th to 18th centuries

by Bert Cargill and James B

RITCHIE
John Ritchie Publishing

40 Beansburn, Kilmarnock, Scotland

ISBN-13: 978 1 910513 86 6

Copyright © 2017 by John Ritchie Ltd.
40 Beansburn, Kilmarnock, Scotland

www.ritchiechristianmedia.co.uk

Typeset by John Ritchie Ltd., Kilmarnock
Printed by Bell & Bain Ltd., Glasgow

TORCHBEARERS OF THE TRUTH

"Blameless and harmless,
the sons of God, without rebuke,
in the midst of a crooked and perverse nation,
among whom ye shine as lights in the world;
holding forth the word of life."

Philippians 2.15-16

Acknowledgements

Many of these accounts have been compiled from information available on websites in the public domain. In addition, individual sources are noted and acknowledged in footnotes throughout the book.

The authors are grateful for access to all of these, as they are to their respective wives for their patience and understanding, and to Christian friends too many to mention for their stimulus and support over many years.

Contents

Preface

This book is being published in 2017, the 500th anniversary year of the start of the Reformation in Europe. It has been written to remind us of the debt we owe to some remarkable servants of God from that distant era, and to others who followed them. They should not be forgotten.

It is not inappropriate nor is it an exaggeration to recognize them as *Torchbearers of the Truth* during 14th to 18th century Great Britain. They led the way out of the darkness of false religion, superstition and ignorance into "the light of the glorious gospel of Christ" (2 Cor 4.4). They did this principally by making available to ordinary people readable copies of the Holy Scriptures and by preaching the Gospel of free grace, both of which have brought light and liberty to countless men and women across the centuries since then.

Our first chapters are therefore about those who pioneered the translation of the Bible into the English language, leading eventually to the 1611 Authorised or 'King James' Version of the Scriptures. Other chapters focus on key figures in the Reformation movement in Europe, England and Scotland, some of whom suffered imprisonment and the pains of martyrdom. We have then selected others who in the 17th and 18th centuries left their mark by how they preached and what they wrote. Some names may not be so well known, but they are included to remind us that God had many faithful servants long before our day, fighting uphill battles often against popular opinions and vested political interests.

We acknowledge that there are many others whose stories are not included here, "of whom the world was not worthy", to quote a phrase from another selection made by a first century writer. For example there are the Scottish Covenanters of the terrible "Killing Times" of 1680-88, who chose extreme hardship and death rather than deny what they firmly believed to be the truth of God's Word. Their stories, and those of many other martyrs, are well told elsewhere.

Most of these chapters are edited versions of a series of articles which first appeared monthly in the *Believer's Magazine* during 2010 to 2012 under the editorship of John Grant whose help and encouragement the authors gratefully acknowledge. They are now being published in this more permanent form for the benefit of a wider readership, to help to keep alive the memory of these worthy servants of God.

A passing knowledge of British history will be helpful in reading this book, so a selective timeline is included for reference in the Appendix.

CHAPTER 1

John Wycliffe (1324 – 1384)

"The Morning Star of the Reformation"

John Wycliffe is chiefly remembered as the person who first gave English speaking people a Bible in their own language. His work was done a century before Gutenberg in Germany invented the printing press, so these Scriptures were hand-written, copied with the help of faithful scribes. The ecclesiastical authorities in their blinded zeal destroyed as many as they could, but even today about 150 complete or partial manuscripts still exist showing how widely distributed and valued they had been.

Wycliffe's Background

John Wycliffe was born at Ipreswell (modern Hipswell) in Yorkshire, around 1324. His family was large and well to do, with an estate called Wycliffe-on-Tees. He probably received his early education near home, but went up to Oxford before 1345, becoming Master of Balliol College by 1360. His university studies were the usual mix of classics, natural science and mathematics, then philosophy. More significant was his deepened interest in Bible study which led to his Bachelor in Theology degree, then Doctor of Theology sometime between 1366 and 1372.

His study Bible was the Latin Vulgate, which was the recognized Bible of the Established Church of the day. Only a few could read it. This Latin version had been translated from the Hebrew and Greek by Jerome and others in the 5th century. But the more Wycliffe studied it, the more it showed up to him the many profound errors in the beliefs and practices of the Church. He felt he had to challenge them. After much spiritual conflict he began to make his revolutionary views known. His conviction was that the Bible alone was authoritative and fully sufficient. Without the knowledge of the Bible, he said, there can be no peace in the life of the Church or of society, and outside of the Bible there is no real and abiding good; it is the one authority for the Christian faith. Thus he recognized and formulated the principle of the Reformation - the unique authority of the Holy Scriptures. The Bible and not the "Church" was the fundamental source of Christian teaching, and this is why he has been called *The Morning Star of the Reformation.*

Translations of the Bible

This conviction was also his motivation for translating the Bible into the English language. He believed more and more that the Bible should be made available for ordinary people to read for themselves in their mother tongue to save them from being misled by a few churchmen who could read it and apply it as they wished. Some of England's nobility possessed a French translation, but no useable English one existed. Wycliffe therefore set himself the great task of translating from the Latin Vulgate into English. It was not all his own work, but it was his initiative. His own translation of the New Testament gave a clearer and more readable text than a version of the Old Testament recently produced by his friend Nicholas of Hereford. When all the translation was completed, the whole Bible was reviewed and revised by Wycliffe's younger associate John Purvey in 1388. This is how the first English Bible was produced. It was written in 'Middle English', a version of the language we would find quite difficult to follow today.

To understand the pivotal role of John Wycliffe in the pre-reformation movement of the 14th century, we need to look at the general conditions in Europe at that time. The Church of Rome held great ecclesiastical and civil power, extending to the appointment of kings and sanctioning the rule of law in many countries. A feudal system was in place, requiring the payment of heavy taxes to Rome, ultimately extorted from the poor. Large and ornate cathedrals had been built, with an elaborate hierarchy of church officials and dignitaries. In monasteries all over Europe various religious orders followed their peculiar levels of asceticism or learning.

Abuses in the Church

Abuses were rife. The Church and its officials were becoming increasingly rich, and many of them including some of the popes were overtly immoral. More and more property and land was being acquired by the Church, all at the expense of a deluded and darkened populace. Generally the medieval scene is one of majestic religious buildings in key locations with elaborate religious rites and ceremonies understood by only a few, alongside spiritual darkness, superstition and poverty among the many. The true Gospel of apostolic days had disappeared and everything was far away from the church described in the New Testament. And social conditions were dreadful – the Black Death was spreading and would soon destroy one third of Europe's population.

A sincere and studious man like Wycliffe quickly saw how vast was the gulf between what the Bible taught about the church and what he saw around him. Theologically, he based his views on a belief in the "invisible" church of the elect, made up of those who are saved, rather than in the "visible" Church of Rome. Wycliffe wrote, "The Church is the totality of those who are predestined to blessedness. It includes the Church triumphant in heaven… and the Church militant or men on earth. No one who is eternally lost has part in it. There is one universal Church, and outside of it there is no salvation. Its head is Christ." He made his views known in written pamphlets and in his preaching and soon deep hostility to him arose in many quarters.

He also insisted that the Church should be poor, as in the days of the apostles. This too aroused controversy and anger as it militated against the vested interests of the religious hierarchy and their financial ambitions. But when he preached in London's churches, the city welcomed him. Some of the nobility attached themselves to him, already envious of the wealth and land ownership of the Church, while the common people gladly heard his sermons, reminiscent of what is said about the Lord Jesus in Mark 12.37.

The Lollards

Wycliffe's vision was to replace existing rich church officials with "poor priests". Bound by no vows, without formal ordination and living in poverty, they would go from place to place preaching the Gospel, *"God's law, without which no one could be justified".* Two by two they went, barefoot, wearing long dark-red robes and carrying a staff, preaching the sovereignty of God in the Gospel. A papal Bull gave them the name of Lollards to disgrace them - but it soon became to them a name of honour as they made the Word of God known far and wide.

It is no surprise that Wycliffe fell foul of the authorities. He was summoned before the bishop of London in February 1377 "to explain the wonderful things which had streamed forth from his mouth". They did not get as far as a definite examination of his case because an angry crowd gathered, party animosities began to appear, fiery exchanges took place and there was a near riot. After this Wycliffe tried to side step the Church authorities by laying his theses before parliament, and then made them public in tracts. He was again called upon to answer at Lambeth Palace in March, 1378. He came ready to conduct his own defence, but a noisy mob gathered intent on saving him. The king's mother, Joan of Kent, also took up his cause. The bishops were divided, and had to be satisfied with formally forbidding him to speak further about these things (as in Acts 4.17–18).

Charges of Heresy

In 1381 Wycliffe set out his doctrine of the Lord's Supper in twelve short sentences, based upon New Testament teaching. The Church hierarchy along with the chancellor of Oxford University pronounced these false and heretical. Wycliffe in turn declared that no one could change his convictions. Instead he published his second great confession upon this subject in English, intended for the common people to hear about through the preaching of the Lollards. Wycliffe's old enemy, Courtenay, now Archbishop of Canterbury, called an ecclesiastical court at London to try him formally. During the consultations an earthquake occurred (21st May, 1382). This terrified the participants who wished to break up the assembled court, but Courtenay declared instead that the earthquake was a sign which favoured the removal of erroneous doctrine from the Church.

Wycliffe's doctrines with reference to transubstantiation and church order were declared heretical and erroneous. To hold these opinions or to advance them in any way was now forbidden and subject to prosecution. Once again Wycliffe was summoned before a synod at Oxford on 18th November, 1382. Although he had suffered a stroke, he was resolute in his defence and earned the favour of the court and of parliament. He was not excommunicated or deprived of his position.

He returned to his base at Lutterworth (near Leicester), and for two more years continued to send out tracts and preach more determinedly about the evils in the Church. While in his parish church on 28th December, 1384, he suffered another stroke, and had to be carried out in his chair. He died just three days later aged about sixty.

42 Years Later

There is a curious addendum to his life story. In 1415, thirty years after his death, a Church Council declared him a stiff-necked heretic and under the ban of the Church. It was decreed that all his books should be burned and his body should be exhumed. It was however another twelve years later until his bones were dug up and burned on the orders of Pope Martin V. In ultimate ignominy, they thought, his ashes were thrown into the River Swift which flows through Lutterworth before entering the River Avon[1].

The influence of John Wycliffe, however, could not be so easily destroyed. He had laid a sure foundation which others would build on, notably William Tyndale who is the subject of our next chapter. He had lit a torch and kindled a fire which would not go out.

BC

Footnote

1. Thomas Fuller, English churchman and historian (1608 – 1661), wrote this about his ashes:

    Thus this brook hath conveyed his ashes into Avon; Avon into Severn; Severn into the narrow seas; they into the main ocean: and thus the ashes of Wickliffe are the emblem of his doctrine, which is now dispersed all the world over.
    (Church History, Book IV, para 53)

    The poet Wm Wordsworth wrote similar lines ending with
    – this deed accurst

    An emblem yields to friends and enemies
    How the bold teacher's doctrine, sanctified
    By truth, shall spread throughout the world dispersed.

CHAPTER 2

William Tyndale (1494 – 1536)

"Architect of the English Language"

Although John Wycliffe had done such pioneering work in making the first English translation of the Bible, William Tyndale is better remembered for his work which followed more than a century later. There are three reasons for this.

His translation is much more accurate, derived directly from Hebrew and Greek texts. Wycliffe translated from the Latin Vulgate, itself rather inaccurate in places, but Tyndale was able to use the Greek New Testament text recently made available in Europe by Erasmus, and also to access some Hebrew texts.

Tyndale's English is nearer our modern form of the language, so that many of his words and phrases remain in versions of the Bible we use today. It has been calculated that in our Authorised Version New Testament 84 % is Tyndale's work, while in the Old Testament 76 % is Tyndale's.

Tyndale was able to take advantage of the printing press, invented by Gutenberg in 1440, with the first Bible printed in Germany in 1452. William Caxton brought the technique to England in 1476. Clearly this facilitated better copies and wider distribution.

Tyndale's Background

William Tyndale was born in 1494 most probably at North Nibley in Gloucestershire. His was an ancient Northumbrian family, perhaps moving there following the Wars of the Roses. At the age of 11 he enrolled at Oxford University, grew up there, and received his Master's Degree in 1515, aged 21. He proved to be a gifted linguist. One of his associates commented that he was "so skilled in eight languages – Hebrew, Greek, Latin, Spanish, French, Italian, English, and German, that whichever he speaks, you might think it his native tongue". Then ordained into the 'priesthood', he was able to start studying theology. His earlier course at Oxford had not included the study of Scripture. He subsequently went up to Cambridge, possibly studying under Erasmus, one of whose books written in Latin in 1503, *The Handbook of the Christian Knight,* he translated into English. Erasmus was one of the most distinguished literary figures of his day. He was prominent in that great revival in Western Europe of Greek and classical studies which resulted from the flight of many Greeks to Italy when the Byzantine Empire had finally collapsed and Constantinople had fallen to the Turks in 1453.

Around 1520, Tyndale became a tutor in the family of Sir John Walsh, at Little Sodbury in Gloucestershire. There he devoted himself more to the study of the Scriptures and embraced the doctrines of the Reformation. His opinions involved him in controversy with his fellow clergymen, and around 1522, he was summoned before the Chancellor of the Diocese of Worcester on a charge of heresy. This led to his move to London (about October 1523), where he continued to preach what he believed to be the truth.

He made many friends among the ordinary people but none among church leaders. A "learned" Roman Catholic clergyman is said to have taunted Tyndale by saying, "We are better to be without God's laws than the Pope's". Tyndale's famous reply was, "I defy the Pope and all his laws. If God spare my life ere many years, I will cause the boy that drives the plow to know more of the scriptures than you!" He was convinced that the way to God was through His word, and that scripture should be made widely available to common people. He said, "Can one imagine a family where the children were unable to understand what their father says?"

Bible Translation

So in London in 1523 he determined to translate the Bible into English. He requested help from Bishop Cuthbert Tunstall, a well-known classicist whom Erasmus had praised after working with him on a Greek New Testament. However, the bishop was suspicious of his theology and, like many highly-placed churchmen, did not like the idea of the Bible in the vernacular. Tyndale preached and studied "at his book" in London for some time, enjoying the help and hospitality of a cloth merchant called Humphrey Monmouth. But as he became more unpopular, he left England under a pseudonym and landed at Hamburg in 1524 taking with him what he had done so far on his translation of the New Testament. He completed this translation in 1525, possibly in Wittenberg, with help from Martin Luther, and also Miles Coverdale and a friar called William Roy.

In 1526 a full edition of the New Testament in English was printed in Worms. More copies were soon being printed in Antwerp, and many were smuggled into England and Scotland where they were to have an abiding influence as we shall see later. It was condemned in October 1526 by Tunstall, who issued dire warnings to booksellers and arranged for copies to be burned in public. Cardinal Wolsey condemned Tyndale as a heretic and demanded his arrest.

Tyndale's other literary activity during this interval was extraordinary. When he left England, his knowledge of Hebrew was very rudimentary and yet he mastered it, so that by 1531, in just seven years, he had produced from the original Hebrew an admirable translation of the entire Pentateuch, the Books of Joshua, Judges, Ruth, First and Second Samuel, First and Second Kings, First Chronicles, and Jonah.

In addition to these he wrote several books and pamphlets about the authority of Scripture and severely critical of established Church practice. All these were written in places so secure and well hidden that the ecclesiastical and diplomatic agents of Wolsey and Henry VIII, charged to hunt him down and seize him, were never able to find him. In 1534, believing that the progress of the Reformation in England made it safe for him to leave his place of hiding, he settled at Antwerp and combined the work of an evangelist with that of a translator of the Bible.

Betrayal and Martyrdom

Tyndale had aroused Henry VIII's anger principally by writing against his divorce. The king asked the emperor Charles V to have Tyndale apprehended and returned to England. Eventually, he was betrayed in Antwerp in 1535 by Henry Phillips, a man he thought was his friend but was actually an agent of Henry and the English ecclesiastics. Tyndale was arrested and imprisoned in the castle of Vilvoorden near Brussels, held there for over 500 days, in horrible, degrading conditions.

In the end he faced a ridiculously unfair trial for heresy and treason, and was condemned to death. He was strangled while tied to the stake, and then his dead body was burned in the prison yard on 6th October, 1536. His last words spoken "at the stake with a fervent zeal, and a loud voice", were reported as *"Lord! Open the King of England's eyes!"*

With this, the voice of a great man aged just 42 was silenced. But his work remained, and his prayer was answered very soon afterwards, for in that very year Henry VIII instigated the Dissolution of the Monasteries and began extensive religious reforms which would include the placing of a Bible in every parish church in England.

Tyndale's Legacy

Tyndale's translation was the foundation of the great translations which quickly followed afterwards. These included the Great Bible of 1539, the Geneva Bible of 1560, the Bishops' Bible of 1568, the Douay-Rheims Bible of 1582–1609, and most notably the Authorised Version of 1611.

About the Authorised Version the Revised Standard Version translators noted: "It kept felicitous phrases and apt expressions, from whatever source, which had stood the test of public usage.

It owed most, especially in the New Testament, to Tyndale." A more recent scholarly review states, "He [Tyndale] is the mainly unrecognised translator of the most influential book in the world. Although the Authorised King James Version is ostensibly the production of a learned committee of churchmen, it is mostly cribbed from Tyndale with some reworking of his translation."

In translating the Bible, Tyndale introduced new words into the English language, many of which have become well loved by today's readers of the AV. For example, it was Tyndale who composed the well known name 'Jehovah' from the Hebrew Tetragrammaton YHWH. He also gave us the Old Testament words *passover, atonement, scapegoat*.

Some of his new words and phrases, however, did not suit the hierarchy of the Roman Catholic Church. They did not want *overseer* to replace their word *bishop*, nor *elder* for their familiar *priest*, nor the more accurate word *congregation* for their word *church*. Tyndale contended (citing Erasmus) that the Greek New Testament did not support those traditional Roman Catholic readings, and history has proved him correct. Yet the influential Thomas More had said that searching for errors in the Tyndale Bible was like searching for water in the sea!

Because of his work on the translation of the Bible, William Tyndale is frequently referred to as the "Architect of the English Language". His influence on English has been as wide and lasting as Shakespeare's.

Many of the phrases which Tyndale coined are in our everyday language. We quote him when we use phrases such as *the powers that be; my brother's keeper; the salt of the earth; a law unto themselves; it came to pass; fight the good fight; the signs of the times.* And when we tell great Bible stories or declare the wonderful message of the Gospel, the familiar words we use are often Tyndale's.

What a legacy he left to us!

BC

CHAPTER 3

Martin Luther (1483 – 1546)

"The just shall live by faith"

The story of Martin Luther, the one time German monk, is the main key to understanding the progress of the Reformation in Europe in the early sixteenth century. Like many others before and after him, it was through studying the Scriptures that divine light dawned on his own soul, and he came to see the grave errors in the powerful Roman Catholic Church. Few have changed the course of history more than he did, releasing Europe from what was tantamount to a huge empire which had ruled its nations by fear for over a thousand years. Luther's influence spread outwards to reach far beyond his own country and his own century, not least because of the recently invented printing press.

Luther's early life

Martin Luther was born to Hans and Margaretha Luder on 10th November, 1483 in Eisleben, Germany. Hans owned a copper mine in nearby Mansfeld, and wanted his son to receive a good education to enable him to enter the civil service. Young Martin attended schools in Mansfeld, Magdeburg and Eisenach but he did not enjoy any of them. When he was seventeen he entered the University of Erfurt. There he did well, receiving his Bachelor's degree after just one year, then a Master's degree three years later, in 1504.

He then entered law school but he found theology and philosophy more interesting than law. He found, however, that philosophy was about the use of reason and had nothing to say about God, which to Luther was more important. Reason could be used to question men and institutions, but not God. He believed that men could learn about God only through divine revelation, and so the Scriptures became increasingly important to him.

About this time, on 2nd July, 1505, while riding back to university after a visit home, he was caught in a terrible thunderstorm and to his horror a lightning bolt narrowly missed him. Terrified of death and divine judgment he called out, "Help! Saint Anna. I will become a monk!" His life was spared, and Luther kept his word and entered the Augustinian monastery in Erfurt two weeks later.

Luther the Monk

In monastic life he made immense efforts to please God by good works. He endured fasts, flagellations, long pilgrimages, and constant confession. Yet he found no peace with God. The more he tried to do, the more he seemed aware of his sinfulness. He would later remark, "If anyone could have gained heaven as a monk, then I would indeed have been among them." He described this period of his life as one of deep spiritual despair. He said, "I lost touch with Christ the Saviour and Comforter, and made of Him the jailor and hangman of my poor soul."

His superior believed that he needed more work to distract him from all this intense introspection and so he was sent off on another academic career. In 1508 he began to teach theology at the University of Wittenberg. He quickly earned his Bachelor's degree in Biblical Studies, and his Doctor of Theology in October 1512.

From 1510 to 1520, as he studied for academic degrees and prepared lectures, he was driven to study the Psalms, Hebrews, Romans, and Galatians in real depth. In so doing he saw that the 'Church' had obscured the central truths of Christianity and indeed was corrupt in its ways. To him the most important doctrine was justification by faith alone. He found peace with God for himself at the well known verse, "The just shall live by faith" (Romans 1.17).

He began to teach publicly that salvation is a gift of God's grace, obtainable only through faith in Christ. He wrote, "This one and firm rock, which we call the doctrine of justification, is the chief article of the whole Christian doctrine, which comprehends the understanding of all godliness." Luther had come to understand justification as entirely the work of God. He wrote that righteousness not only comes from Christ but actually is the righteousness of Christ, imputed to believers through faith.

He explained his concept of justification as follows:

"The first and chief article is this: Jesus Christ, our God and Lord, died for our sins and was raised again for our justification (Romans 3.24–25). He alone is the Lamb of God who takes away the sins of the world (John 1.29), and God has laid on Him the iniquity of us all (Isaiah 53.6). All have sinned and are justified freely, without their own works and merits, by His grace, through the redemption that is in Christ Jesus, in His blood (Romans 3.23–25). This is necessary to believe. This cannot be otherwise acquired or grasped by any work, law or merit. Therefore, it is clear and certain that this faith alone justifies us ... Nothing of this article can be yielded or surrendered, even though heaven and earth and everything else falls (Mark 13.31)."

The 95 Theses

Things reached a crisis point for Luther when Johann Tetzel came to Germany to sell 'Indulgences' to raise funds to rebuild St Peter's Basilica in Rome. Indignant at both the exploitation of the poor and the errors of the Church, he did what he is best remembered for. He wrote his *95 Theses* condemning the practices of the Roman Catholic Church. He posted them on the door of the Church of All Saints in Wittenberg on 31st October 1517. Before long they were translated from Latin into German, printed, and widely copied. Within two weeks, they had spread throughout Germany; within two months throughout Europe.

Luther's views were of course condemned as heretical by Pope Leo X in 1520. He was summoned to either renounce or reaffirm them at the famous *Diet of Worms* on 17th April 1521. When he appeared before the Diet, he was asked if he still believed what he had written. He requested time to think about his answer. He prayed, consulted with friends and the next day in front of the Diet he apologized for the harsh tone of many of his writings, but respectfully and boldly stated, "Unless I am convinced by proofs from Scriptures or by plain and clear reasons and arguments, I can and will not retract, for it is neither safe nor wise to do anything against conscience. God help me. Amen." On 25th May, the Emperor issued his Edict, declaring Martin Luther an outlaw. This made it a crime for anyone in Germany to give Luther food or shelter, and permitted anyone to kill him without legal consequence.

But Luther had some powerful friends among the princes of Germany. One of them, Frederick the Wise, Elector of Saxony, arranged for him to be seized on his way from the Diet by a company of masked horsemen. They carried him to safety in the castle of Wartburg where he lived for a year. He called this 'my Patmos'. During this period he worked hard at his translation of the Bible.

He was the first person to translate and publish the Bible in the commonly-spoken dialect of the German people. He used the recent 1516 critical Greek edition of Erasmus (later called *textus receptus)*. The German New Testament was published in September 1522; the Old Testament followed in 1534.

A staunch ally and supporter of Luther was Philip Melanchthon (1497-1560). He came to Wittenberg University in 1518 as professor of Greek, and there Luther taught him theology while he taught Luther Greek. He then encouraged and assisted Luther in his translation of the Greek New Testament; with his great literary abilities he wrote extensively in support of the Reformation. A friendship between these men developed which lasted until Luther's death. Melanchthon gave the oration at Luther's funeral, and fourteen years later was buried next to him.

Luther wrote many other books and pamphlets. Between 1518 and 1525 he published more of these than most of the reformers combined. He wrote many hymns, his best known one is *A Mighty Fortress is Our God*. His 1524 hymn *We All Believe in One True God* is a three-stanza confession of faith based on "The Apostles' Creed".

Later life

On 13th June 1525 he married 26 year old Katharina von Bora. She was one of twelve nuns he had helped to escape from a Cistercian convent in 1523, getting them smuggled out hidden inside herring barrels! They had a happy and successful marriage, though money was often short. Katharina helped the family income by farming and taking in boarders. They had six children, four of whom lived to adulthood.

Luther's ideas were sometimes taken to extremes and out of context. He had to return to Wittenberg in 1522 to rebuke those who tried to stir up revolt against the ruling classes in Germany. He insisted on the practice of Christian values such as love, patience, charity, and freedom, and reminded the protestors to trust God's Word rather than use violence to bring about change. In the Peasants' War of 1524–25 many atrocities were committed often in Luther's name. Whilst sympathising with the peasants' real grievances over exploitation, he reminded them of their duty to obey authorities. He explained what the Bible taught about wealth, and at the same time condemned violence as the devil's work.

Sad to say, Luther did not get all his doctrines correct. After some attempts to show kindness to already persecuted Jews because, he said, Jesus Christ was born a Jew, he became very bitter against them. He wrote some things in 1543 which can only be described now as anti-Semitic, denying that they were God's chosen people. In mitigation, some have noted that Luther was then in deteriorating health and his mind may have been affected. He died of a heart attack on 18th February 1546, aged 62, in Eisleben where he had been born.

Luther's influence was immense. He befriended William Tyndale during his exile in 1525, and gave him the use of his own 1516

Erasmus Greek-Latin Parallel New Testament. This would lead to Tyndale's English New Testament of 1525-26. Likewise in 1544 he encouraged the exiled Scotsmen George Wishart and John Knox and showed them the way forward which they adhered to. These, and countless others since, followed the path that this man of God had shown out of darkness and superstition into the light and liberty of the Gospel. His text, "The just shall live by faith", is as precious and influential as ever.

Reformation Day

The Reformation in Europe finds its origin in Luther's stance against the Roman Catholic Church, and particularly his *95 Theses* nailed to the church door at Wittenberg on 31st October 1517. This date is called Reformation Day and is celebrated annually as a public holiday in Germany and many other European countries. 31st October 2017 is the 500th anniversary of this seminal event.

BC

CHAPTER 4

John Calvin (1509 – 1564)

In the Reformation in Europe, Martin Luther and John Calvin are both recognised as key figures. It is sometimes claimed that Calvin's influence was greater than Luther's especially in their effects in Scotland and England, but this is hard to prove and may depend on one's own bias. What is clear from history is that the spiritual legacy of each was most significant, lasting to this day. Their lives overlapped, although Calvin was born twenty six years after Luther, and lived fifty five years compared to Luther's sixty three.

Luther in Germany pursued the Reformation cause with boldness, never shrinking from public disputes and fearless preaching (see Chapter 3), much as John Knox would do later in Scotland. Calvin was a more reticent man, of a studious disposition, equally convinced of the need for reform and the reasons for it, but more withdrawn and contemplative. His lasting gift to the church is in his writings, particularly *The Institutes of the Christian Religion,* the first short edition of which he wrote at the age of twenty six. Sadly, his name has been exploited by attaching to it an –*ism*, which in its more extreme versions has done the cause of the Gospel much harm, and which it is most probable that Calvin would have distanced himself from. How tragic that the history of the church has been beset so much with –*isms* and hero worship and consequent schisms, even from the days when 1 Corinthians 1.12 was written.

In France

John Calvin was born on 10th July 1509, firstly named Jehan

Cauvin, at Noyon, in Picardy, 60 miles northeast of Paris, the first of four sons who survived infancy. His mother, Jeanne le Franc, the daughter of an innkeeper, died when Jehan was about six years old. His father, Gérard Cauvin, was a prosperous cathedral official.

Young Calvin was a precocious lad, and was influenced by his father to seek an academic career and to become a lawyer. At the age of twelve he went to college in Paris where he learned Latin and the less fashionable Greek, then to a strict and severe monastery school, thence to the universities of Orleans and Bourges to study law. However, he became more interested in philosophy and humanism. The death of his father in 1531 gave him the opportunity to pursue his interests in the humanities at Paris, and by 1533 he had written a thesis on Seneca's *De Clementia*.

Reformation teaching was getting to Paris at this time, and Calvin, along with several other students and teachers, was attracted to it. But the authorities were not, in fact they vehemently opposed it, and that group had to disperse for their safety. Calvin went to the south of France under a pseudonym, and then left France to settle in the German town of Basel. It was in 1533 during this time of uncertainty that he was truly converted. He wrote, "God by a sudden conversion subdued and brought my mind to a teachable frame", seeing it as much a change from ignorance to knowledge as from condemnation to justification[1].

In Geneva

Because of the hostile situation in France he decided to move permanently into Germany and settle at Strasbourg. He was not able to take the direct route to Strasbourg because of the war between France under Francis I and the Holy Roman Empire under Charles V, so he had to make a detour via Geneva for an overnight stop. But that night he was recognised by Guillaume Farel,[2] who forcefully persuaded him to stay and help the work of the Reformation which was just beginning in Geneva. Now aged thirty, he would remain there for the rest of his life apart from a short exile during 1538 – 1541 when he ministered in a church in Strasbourg.

Recalled to Geneva he became recognised as both a theologian and a preacher. He set out to achieve the separation of the church from civil and state control over matters of discipline, but not without difficulty. He organised daily meetings for singing Psalms and learning Scripture, he opened schools for the poor and hospitals for the sick, particularly when plague seriously affected the city and he personally risked infection by his visitations. By different means he attempted to organise a city which would operate on scriptural principles, owning God as sovereign and authoritative, effectively a theocracy.

Later controversies were not always settled amicably however. An unhappy example is that of Michael Severitus, a Spanish theologian whose beliefs were deemed to be heretical (and we would think they were). After lengthy correspondence with Calvin and a growing reputation for his errors, he was condemned to death by burning by a court in France, but escaped from his prison. He came to Geneva to visit Calvin in spite of having such a reputation, but brought before a court the earlier verdict was confirmed and Severitus was burnt at the stake on the outskirts of Geneva in 1553.

In 1540 John Calvin married a widow, Idelette de Bure. He had been urged by his friends to marry before this to exemplify the protestant view of marriage rather than appear to favour the Romish one of celibacy. He resisted their wishes even when a suitable lady was found for him, saying he would not marry her "unless the Lord had entirely bereft me of my wits". The eventual marriage was a happy one, lasting for nine years, during which a son Jacques was born prematurely in 1542. Sadly he had the grief of seeing that little one die soon after. His words at that time of grief are poignant and memorable: "God is Himself a Father, and knows what is best for His children." Idelette fell ill three years later and died on 29th March 1549. Calvin never married again. He expressed his sorrow in a letter: "I have been bereaved of the best friend of my life, of one who, if it had been so ordained, would willingly have shared not only my poverty but also my death. During her life she was the faithful helper of my ministry. From her I never experienced the slightest hindrance."

The Preacher and Writer

His time in Geneva was devoted to teaching, preaching and writing. He taught classes three times a week, preached daily every other week, and in 1540 began to write commentaries on books of the Bible, a project which eventually included almost all of them. Latterly his sermons were recorded in shorthand and put into print so that they are still accessible. His preaching in St Peter's Church was passionate and effective. He preached without notes, with simplicity and passion. It was said to be biblical, sequential, exegetical, pastoral and accessible to all. And it was evangelical, as was Calvin's attitude to missions. He did believe in "whosoever will may come" and showed his beliefs in his actions. In Geneva, many hundreds of preachers were trained by him and went to other countries with the Gospel, notably to his native France where it is estimated that 2,150 underground churches were planted between 1560 and 1562, some with thousands in their congregations.

He revised and enlarged his *Institutes* in 1539, 1543, 1550, and finally in 1559, by which time it had grown from 85,000 words in six chapters to 450,000 words in four books of eighty chapters each. Its central theme is that the sum of human wisdom consists of two parts: the knowledge of God and of ourselves. He argues that the knowledge of God is not inherent and it cannot be discovered by observing this world. The only way to obtain it is to study the Scriptures: "For anyone to arrive at God the Creator he needs Scripture as his Guide and Teacher". His *Institutes of the Christian Religion* was (and to many it still is) the most complete account and defence of the protestant faith, scripture-based with quotations to support all its propositions. It emphasised the then controversial but critical doctrine that the authority of the Scriptures is above that of the Church.

His commentaries were written in such a way as to make the

text of scripture real as the Word of God to man. He would focus his mind on the writer of the book and thereby clarify the plain meaning of the text for his readers. Explanation, however, was not the end of the matter, it was for the edification of the reader. He did not use allegorical interpretation but focused on literal meanings as much as possible. In all his commentaries he uses his *Institutes* as the reference material, saving him from frequent repetition of fundamental doctrines each time.

Final Days

In the autumn of 1558, Calvin became ill with a fever. He had suffered previous spells of illness due to overwork and also episodes with kidney stones. This time, afraid that he might die before completing the final revision of his book, he forced himself to work. Shortly afterwards he recovered, but straining his voice by preaching brought on violent coughing which burst a blood vessel in his lungs. His health steadily deteriorated thereafter, and he preached his final sermon in St. Peter's on 6th February 1564.

On 25th April, he made his will in which he left some money to his family and to the college in Geneva. He died on 27th May 1564 and was buried the next day in an unmarked grave in the Cimetière des Rois. He had explicitly stated in his will that such an unmarked burial place should be his for he did not want any risk of hero worship to follow him and obscure the glory of God. The exact location of the grave is not known, but a stone was added in the 19th century to mark a grave traditionally thought to be his.

Some aspects of John Calvin's life, and some points of the doctrine which he is said to have fostered, may not be the kind of thing which we enjoy or even agree with, especially in the overemphasised and exaggerated forms promoted by others since his day. But it is fairly clear that John Calvin was a man with a humble opinion of himself, who pursued the knowledge of God theologically and practically, who put God first in his life, and influenced thousands in his day towards Christ and true Christianity. He showed how Christianity extended beyond church buildings, that it went away beyond the preaching and hearing of sermons, that bringing the Gospel to others required contact with them while keeping separate from worldly ways and pursuits. In these things he was more than a torchbearer in the past - he is still a role model for us today.

BC

Footnotes

1. *John Calvin, a Heart for Devotion, Doctrine and Doxology,* Ed B Parsons, Reformation Trust, 2008, was published to mark the 500th anniversary of his birth.

2. Guillaume or William Farel was 20 years older than Calvin. He had embraced Luther's teaching and had fearlessly preached the Gospel. It is said that he possessed the fiery spirit of a latter day Elijah. In danger of his life he fled from France to Switzerland in 1524.

CHAPTER 5

Patrick Hamilton (1504 – 1528)

The First of the Scottish Reformation Martyrs

On a cold windswept afternoon on the last day of February 1528, the first and the youngest of the Scottish martyrs of the Reformation period was burned at the stake in the old university town of St Andrews.[1] You can still see the spot where it happened, preserved by his initials PH marked out in the cobble-stones by the gate of St Salvator's College in North Street.[2] Patrick Hamilton was only 24 years old.

St Andrews with its grand cathedral and its castle was at that time the foremost seat and centre of the Roman Catholic Church in Scotland. In that city by the sea, Archbishop James Beaton watched the young Hamilton fearlessly preaching the doctrines of the Gospel which he had learned from Luther in Germany. Alarmed and annoyed, Beaton soon had him accused and condemned as a heretic to suffer a heretic's death. This became one of the main catalysts for the great spiritual changes shortly to come upon Scotland during the sixteenth century.

How did he achieve so much in such a short life? His story is full of interest.

Noble Background

First, unlike most of the later 17th century martyrs of the Scottish Covenanter movement, Patrick Hamilton was of noble and royal blood. His father, Sir Patrick Hamilton was a nephew of King James IV who was killed at the ill fated battle of Flodden Field in 1513. His mother Catherine Stewart was the granddaughter of King James II. Thus Patrick Hamilton the martyr was a great great-grandson of a Scottish king.

He was probably born on his father's estate at Stonehouse in Lanarkshire, and educated at Linlithgow. At the age of thirteen, he was given the nominal title of Abbot of Fearn Abbey in Ross-shire, and was sent to the University of Paris and supported there on the income from that title. He obtained the degree of Master of the Arts at the age of sixteen.

The writings of Martin Luther were being publicly debated at the Sorbonne in Paris while Hamilton was a student. The authorities condemned them as heretical and ordered them to be burned. In the debate, Hamilton, a young man of great intellect and honesty, came to the decision that Luther's doctrines were correct because they were based on the Scriptures. To confirm his convictions he moved to Holland for a short spell to study under Erasmus, the great scholar who had laboured to construct a single continuous text of the Greek New Testament. In 1523 he returned to Scotland and joined the Faculty of Arts at St Andrews University where he found freedom to teach and also assist in cathedral services.

At this time Luther's books were reaching Scotland, smuggled into east coast ports such as Aberdeen, Leith and St Andrews, sometimes hidden inside bales of cloth. The church hierarchy was now on edge because these were becoming so widely accepted throughout the country. With the authority of King James V, a 14-year old boy manipulated by the church authorities, the books were banned as 'damnable opinions of heresy', with severe penalties for possession. To add to their concerns, traders from Leith, Dundee, and Montrose had obtained Tyndale's English New Testament ('recently invented by Martin Luther' some monks declared), and were selling copies in Edinburgh and St. Andrews.

Danger Signals

Against this background, Hamilton found many people willing to listen to him as he openly taught what was based upon the Bible and not the dogma of the Church. Soon however, he was called into question by Archbishop Beaton. This led to a formal summons and an accusation of heresy with a predictable outcome. For safety, Hamilton fled to Germany in April 1527, almost ten years after Luther's courageous actions had begun the Reformation. When he arrived in Wittenberg he found to his delight that the Reformation was not just a series of doctrinal statements - monasteries were deserted, priests had married, and the people were joyfully singing Christian hymns.

In Wittenburg and then Marburg his faith was nurtured and his convictions deepened, expressed in a series of thirteen doctrinal theses called *Patrick's Places*.[3] In these he clearly set out the differences between law and grace, and described justification by faith and the sufficiency of the work of Christ alone for salvation.

Many urged him to stay on in Marburg, but he felt the call to be a light in the darkness of his native Scotland. So he returned in the autumn of 1527. His first converts were his mother, brother and sister, some other members of his family at Kincavel, then others in the next parish of Linlithgow. He married a young lady of noble rank and they had a daughter called Isabel. One reason for his marriage he said was to expose the hypocrisy of the celibacy of monks.

But in Beaton's view, he was a dangerous heretic. His biographer says: "A Lutheran missionary, with royal blood in his veins, and all the power of the Hamiltons at his back, was a more formidable heretic in Scotland than Luther himself would have been".[3] So Patrick was invited to a conference in St Andrews. He told his friends that he believed he had not long to live. Arriving in mid January 1528 he was given liberty to preach and teach while Beaton and his men listened and plotted. They arranged debates in which they vainly tried to convince the young man of his errors, one Alexander Alane being especially fervent in this effort.

When persuasion failed, force took over. His friends urged him to flee, but he refused saying this was why he had come. He preached more earnestly in the short time he had left. Early in the dark morning of 29th February Patrick Hamilton was called to a hastily arranged church council in St Andrews cathedral. His thirteen articles were read out and he was asked to deny them or confirm them. One famous reply was, "I say with Paul, 'There is no mediator betwixt God and man but Christ Jesus, His Son'; and whatsoever they be who call or pray to any saint departed, they spoil Christ Jesus of His office." Confidently and ably he confirmed all that he had written. He was condemned to death without delay. News of all this had reached his brother Sir James Hamilton, and by this time he was actually on his way to rescue him by force, but a storm blew up in the Firth of Forth and delayed him.

Martyrdom

At noon the prisoner was taken and chained to the stake surrounded by faggots and gunpowder. Before a large crowd of witnesses he was given a last chance to deny what he had so courageously confessed, and obtain his life. Calmly and with dignity he maintained his stand for the truth.

So the fire was kindled. Some gunpowder exploded, but the wind and the rain put the fire out, prolonging his suffering. Three more attempts had to be made with fresh combustibles before the terrible act was concluded by 6pm that fateful evening. His last words were: "How long, Lord, shall darkness overwhelm this kingdom? How long wilt Thou suffer this tyranny of men? Lord Jesus, receive my spirit!"

The effect of Patrick Hamilton's martyrdom would be far reaching. One of his first converts was the Alexander Alane (Alesius) who had debated vigorously with him only weeks before. Alane fled to Germany and became a key figure in support of the reformation there and in England. He carried with him these eye witness accounts of Hamilton's martyrdom which have survived to appear here.

Another was Henry Forrest, a young monk who spoke out in favour of Patrick Hamilton and his beliefs. He was thrown into prison and sentenced to be burnt. When his execution was being discussed, John Lindsay, one of Beaton's men, advised that Forrest be burned in some cellar; "For," said he, *"the reek of Patrick Hamilton hath infected all those on whom it blew."* Indeed it did, but in 1533, this other martyr was secretly suffocated.

Serious questions now arose in the minds of many others far and near. Why should so young a man, and a man of noble lineage, suffer in this way and with such dignity? Was what he lived and died for actually true?

Patrick Hamilton became the historical and spiritual link between Martin Luther on the continent (1483 – 1546) and John Knox in Scotland (1510 – 1572). The next link would be George Wishart (1513 – 1546) also martyred in St Andrews only 18 years later as we shall see in the next chapter. These courageous torchbearers of the truth were "faithful unto death", to pass on to others and eventually to us the knowledge of the way of salvation and eternal life through faith in Christ.

BC

Footnotes

1. The first martyr in St Andrews was actually pre-reformation. Paul Craw, a Czech Hussite and Lollard, was burned at St Andrews market cross in 1433 for spreading Wycliffe's translation of the Bible. A cross in the cobble-stones marks that spot also.

2. For hundreds of years up to the present day, students of St Andrews University by tradition avoid stepping on the PH anagram on the pavement.

3. More details about "Patrick's Places" and of his short life in *Patrick Hamilton, The First Lutheran Preacher and Martyr of Scotland* by William Dallmann, 1918.

CHAPTER 6

George Wishart (1513 – 1546)

"Suffer patiently for the Gospel's sake"

George Wishart arrived on the scene of pre-reformation Scotland at a critical time. A biography of Wishart begins thus: "The martyrdom at St Andrews ... of Patrick Hamilton ... sufficiently proved that, in the maintenance of its supremacy, the Roman Church was determined to strike everywhere. But the death of this amiable martyr, instead of repressing ... induced further investigation into the working of a system, maintained by the sale of indulgences on the one hand, and upheld by the executioner on the other."[1] George Wishart was to advance this further investigation and also authenticate it by his own martyrdom in St Andrews.

Early Life

He was born in 1513 at Pitarrow, near Montrose on the east coast of Scotland, the only son of James Wishart, a justice-clerk to King James V. He studied at the University of Leuven and graduated in 1531, well qualified in the Greek language. He returned to teach Greek at Montrose in a school established by John Erskine of Dun, using as his textbook copies of the Greek New Testament which he distributed among his pupils. This was reported to John Hepburn, Bishop of nearby Brechin, who in 1538 summonsed him on investigation of a charge of heresy. It was a crime to read the New Testament in its original language!

He fled to Cambridge where he was able to study and teach, then to Bristol where his preaching aroused opposition from

Archbishop Thomas Cranmer. He then recanted some of his statements, escaping death by 'burning his faggot'. He returned to Germany and visited Switzerland where his commitment to Luther's teaching was reinforced, before returning to Cambridge in 1542. At that university he was noted for his humble, godly and charitable lifestyle.

He returned again to Scotland in July 1543, assured of the protection of some noblemen who were in alliance with the king of England and had actually made plans to assassinate Cardinal David Beaton. (He had been appointed Cardinal in 1539 following the death of his uncle, the James Beaton of St Andrews who was responsible for the martyrdom of Patrick Hamilton.) Wishart spent some time in secret at his native Pitarrow, but could not rest from his urge to evangelise Scotland. So he went and preached to large audiences in Montrose and Dundee, then in the west of Scotland, including Ayr, Galston, Bar and Mauchline.

Dundee and St Andrews

While he was in the west he heard that the plague was raging in Dundee. He hurried back, and surrounded by disease and misery he preached from the text, "He sent His word and healed them" (Ps 107.20); adding, "It is neither herb nor plaster, O Lord, but Thy word healeth all." Standing at the East Port of the stricken city (later called the Wishart Arch which is still standing in the old part of Dundee) he was heard by the victims banished outside and the still healthy people inside. Staying on he visited the sick and preached God's Word.

All of this did not escape the attention of Beaton only 11 miles away in St Andrews. He arranged for a Dundee priest to assassinate Wishart with a dagger as he came down from his pulpit one day. But Wishart saw him first and disarmed him. The crowd called for the assassin's death, who was now begging for mercy, but Wishart restrained them and let the man go free. Later he evaded an ambush to capture him on a journey to one of his friends. It was now clear that his life was in danger, so from then on he never moved about without a bodyguard and a strong man carrying a two-handed sword. As we shall see in the next chapter, John Knox was the last person to do this for him.

From Dundee he was invited to Edinburgh by some of his supporters, where they intended to have a public debate with the bishops. This did not materialise but he found opportunities to preach to large audiences in Leith, Inveresk, Tranent, and Haddington at the end of 1545. On one occasion when only a few turned up to hear him he cried, "O Lord, how long shall it be that Thy holy Word shall be despised, and men shall not regard their own salvation?" For a few months he lived in Brunstain, Longniddry, and Ormiston, with gentlemen who supported the Reformation cause.

He knew he was a wanted man in mortal danger. With his host John Cockburn he left Haddington to go to Ormiston for the last time. John Knox, his defender, wished to accompany him but he said, "Nay, return to your bairns, and God bless you; one is sufficient for one sacrifice."

The Provincial Synod had met at Edinburgh on 13th January, but Beaton adjourned it till after Easter, promising that in the interval he would "put to silence a heretic who was giving him much concern by disturbing the Church". Shortly thereafter, along with the Earl of Bothwell as local Sheriff, Beaton had the house of Ormiston surrounded by troops at midnight and ordered Cockburn and his guests to surrender. Bothwell promised Wishart that he would be kept safe in his custody. Wishart said, "Open the gates, the blessed will of my God be done."

Bothwell took Wishart to Elphinstone Tower on 16th January while John Cockburn and other sympathisers were sent to Edinburgh Castle. Cockburn later escaped by miraculously climbing down the sheer face of the castle wall. Bothwell soon abandoned his promises and delivered Wishart to the governor of Edinburgh Castle. After a few days, he was removed by Cardinal Beaton to his own castle in St Andrews, and there confined for four weeks in the notorious dark 'bottle dungeon' in the sea-tower.

On 28th February, Beaton along with Archbishop Dunbar of Glasgow and all the Scottish bishops met in St Andrews cathedral. Armed men brought the prisoner. At the gate of the cathedral he threw his purse to a beggar, saying that he would no longer need it. After an address by Winram, a church dignitary, George Wishart was given the opportunity to reply and defend himself. He did so with dignity but was railed on and defamed at every turn.

Martyrdom at the stake

As expected, the bishops returned a verdict of "guilty". Wishart, on his knees, prayed, "Gracious and everlasting God, how long wilt Thou permit Thy servants to suffer through infatuation and ignorance? We know that the righteous must suffer persecution in this life, which passeth as doth a shadow, yet we would entreat Thee, merciful Father, that Thou wouldest defend Thy people whom Thou hast chosen, and give them grace to endure and continue in Thy Holy Word."

The cardinal sentenced the prisoner to be burned to ashes. The execution was fixed for the next day, 1st March, 1546. A stake was erected in the centre of an open space in front of the castle. At the front windows the cardinal and bishops reclined on sumptious cushions while two executioners brought out the prisoner. They dressed him in black linen, hung bags of gunpowder around him then led him to his death.

At the stake, Wishart fell upon his knees, and loudly prayed: "Saviour of the world, have mercy upon me. Heavenly Father, into Thy hands I commend my spirit." To the crowd he said: "Christian brethren and sisters, be not offended at the Word of God on account of the tortures you see prepared for me. Love the Word which publisheth salvation, and suffer patiently for the Gospel's sake. To my brethren and sisters who have heard me elsewhere, declare that my doctrine is no old wife's fables, but the blessed Gospel of salvation. For preaching that Gospel, I am now to suffer, and I suffer gladly for the Redeemer's sake. Should any of you be called on to endure persecution, fear not them who can destroy the body, for they cannot slay the soul. I believe that my soul shall sup with my Saviour this night."

He prayed for those who had accused and condemned him. One of the executioners asked his forgiveness. He kissed him on the cheek, saying, "By this token I forgive thee; do thine office." Now tied to the stake, a heap of faggots was piled around his body, the fire was lit and amid the explosions and the flames he left this world and entered the joy of his Lord.

Endpiece

"The triumphing of the wicked is short" (Job 20.5). Three months later, on 29th May a band of Fife men led by Norman and John Leslie cunningly gained access to Beaton's castle and murdered him. They stripped him, and his disfigured body hung for weeks from the very window where he had watched the dying agonies of George Wishart.

And in that very castle soon afterwards, in 1547, the first congregation of the Protestant Church in Scotland was meeting, with John Knox among them.

BC

Footnote

1. *Life of George Wishart the Scottish Martyr*, by Charles Rogers, 1876

CHAPTER 7

John Knox (1510 – 1572)

"Give me Scotland or I die."

Of all those who promoted the Reformation with its insistence upon the authority of the Scriptures and justification by faith alone, in Scotland no name is better known than that of John Knox. An influential figure with a gift of fiery oratory, it is said that "churchmen and monarchs alike came to resent and fear Knox's words". He had frequent and hostile encounters with both throughout his public life. A contemporary wrote, "I assure you that the voice of this one man is able in one hour to put more life into us than five hundred trumpets continually blasting in our ears."

Early Influences

John Knox was born around 1510 in or near Haddington, East Lothian. His father, William Knox, a peasant farmer, is said to have fought for Scotland's king in the ill fated battle of Flodden in 1513. His mother died when he was a young boy. After his education near home, he went up to St Andrews University from which he graduated in 1540. From then to 1543 he acted as a Roman Catholic priest in St Andrews, but did not pursue many parish duties. Instead he became a tutor to influential families back in his native East Lothian where interest was stirring in the new protestant religion.

At this time, George Wishart, probably the pioneer evangelist of the Scottish Reformation, arrived in East Lothian as we noted in Chapter 6. Knox became one of his converts and closest associates. He accompanied him abroad to Geneva in 1544 where he was greatly influenced by John Calvin and Martin Luther. He called Geneva under Calvin "the most perfect school of Christ since the apostles".

Knox eventually became Wishart's bodyguard, carrying a huge two-handed sword to defend him against assassination threats. When Wishart was arrested in December 1545, soon after to be burned at the stake in front of St Andrews Castle on the orders of Cardinal Beaton, Knox was prepared to follow him, but Wishart said, "Nay, return to your bairns and God bless you. One is sufficient for a sacrifice." This, and his first-hand knowledge of the 1528 martyrdom of Patrick Hamilton in St Andrews, made deep impressions on Knox. His course was set.

Knox and St Andrews

After Beaton was killed and St Andrews Castle taken by the reformers, Knox returned there with his young pupils in April 1547. He became chaplain to the garrison in that very castle. Soon his powerful preaching was being heard by large congregations in St Andrews, proclaiming the authority of the Bible and not the Church, and salvation by grace through faith. Hearers enthused by the fiery preaching ransacked the cathedral and smashed statues and images. A bit later the same happened in Perth.

Knox's peace in St Andrews was not to last very long. Mary of Guise, the queen regent, enlisted the help of the king of France to retake the castle. On 29th June 1547, French galleys sailed into St Andrews Bay, the castle was besieged and it surrendered on 31st July. The protestant defenders, including Knox, were taken prisoner, to spend nineteen months as galley slaves, chained to oars, watched over by an officer with a whip in hand. They were threatened with torture if they did not give proper reverence when mass was performed on the ship. Knox recounted an incident in which one Scot was being forced to give a kiss of veneration to a picture of the Virgin Mary. When it was pushed up to his face, he threw it away into the water. After that, according to Knox, the prisoners were no longer forced into such spurious devotions.

In 1548, the French galleys returned to Scotland to scout for English ships. Knox was ill with a fever and on the ship they feared for his life. But his mind remained sharp, and focused on hopes of release. While the ships were lying at anchor in St Andrews Bay, James Balfour, a fellow prisoner, asked Knox if he recognised the landmark spire of the parish church. He replied, "I see the steeple of that place where God first opened my mouth to His glory; and I am fully persuaded, how weak soever I now appear, that I shall not depart this life till my tongue shall glorify His godly name in that same place." His words came true.

Away from Scotland and back again

He was released in February 1549 and took refuge in England, by then more protestant minded. He was given preaching responsibilities in churches in Berwick-on-Tweed, in Newcastle, and then in Buckinghamshire. But in 1554, a new queen, Mary Tudor, re-established Roman Catholicism in England and it was no longer safe for protestant preachers such as Knox to remain. He fled through France to Geneva once more where he settled briefly, preaching there and in Frankfurt.

He returned to Scotland for a year and with the support of many influential nobles was able to preach openly in Edinburgh in spite of the antagonism of Mary of Guise and her bishops. At this time he married Marjorie Bowes, then went back to Geneva on 13th September 1556 where his two sons, Nathaniel and Eleazar, were born. He preached and wrote several books and pamphlets, which are renowned for their forthrightness and zeal.

Knox's next return to Scotland in May 1559 was to a scene of great turmoil. Political and religious controversy was raging between followers of Mary of Guise and many of the Scottish nobles. Mary declared Knox an outlaw, but he found refuge in Dundee and Perth, and eventually again in St Andrews. On 30th June, the reformers occupied Edinburgh, and on 1st July, Knox preached from the pulpit of St Giles' cathedral. Many of his sermons clearly declare the way of salvation through faith in Christ alone by the efficacy of His blood. They are accessible along with much more information about these turbulent times in his major literary work, *The History of the Reformation in Scotland*.[1] On 24th October, the Scottish nobility deposed Mary of Guise from the regency. She died suddenly in Edinburgh Castle on 10th June 1560, and at last French and English troops withdrew from Scotland. On 19th July Knox led a national Thanksgiving Service at St Giles.

In August 1560, the Scottish Parliament accepted the reformed 'confession of faith' drawn up by Knox and others. Three acts were passed in one day:

> to abolish the jurisdiction of the Pope in Scotland,

> to condemn all doctrine and practice contrary to the reformed faith,

> to forbid the celebration of the Mass in Scotland.

Mary, Queen of Scots

A year later, a new queen arrived in Edinburgh, the legendary Mary, Queen of Scots, aged eighteen, whose mother had been her regent in Scotland. Mary had lived her life in France and was a convinced Romanist. She came to face up to the man who was more the leader of her people than she could be.

In his *History*, Knox records five 'conversations' with the queen. They were more rebukes and ultimatums, while she flattered Knox and tried to win him with her tears. In her private chapel she was restoring the Mass which Parliament had outlawed, her paramours and adulteries were well known, she married her second husband's presumed murderer – all of which led to her downfall. After five years in Edinburgh, she abdicated, was imprisoned on an island in the middle of Loch Leven, and eventually escaped to England, leaving her infant son James as king of Scotland. Knox would see to it that James was brought up as a Protestant.

Latter Years

In December 1560, Knox's wife, Marjorie, had died, leaving him to care for their two young sons. In March 1564, controversially, he married Margaret Stewart, seventeen years old, and a distant relative of the deposed queen. They had three daughters, Martha, Margaret, and Elizabeth.

The conflict in Scotland continued. Knox chose to leave Edinburgh and return to St Andrews for a time where he again preached, lectured to students, and worked on his *History*. At the end of July 1572, after a truce was called, he returned to Edinburgh, although by this time he was very feeble and his voice faint. On 9th November he inducted a new minister in St Giles.

His last day on earth was 24th November. With his friends and some of the greatest Scottish nobles around him, he asked his young wife to read to him. "Go, read where I cast my first anchor," he said. It was John chapter 17.

Afterwards she read Psalm 9, applicable to his lifetime and ours:

> The wicked shall be turned into hell, and all the nations that forget God. For the needy shall not alway be forgotten: the expectation of the poor shall not perish for ever. Arise, O Lord; let not man prevail: let the heathen be judged in thy sight. Put them in fear, O Lord: that the nations may know themselves to be but men.

He was buried in St Giles' graveyard, his grave now beneath the car park behind the cathedral. It is marked by a small stone plaque set in the tarmac near the centre at space number 23. A large funeral procession followed the body to its last resting-place and heard the new regent of Scotland, James Douglas, Earl of Morton, declare, "Here lyeth a man who in his life never feared the face of man, ... yet hath ended his dayes in peace and honour."

John Knox claimed in his will, *None have I corrupted, none have I defrauded; merchandise have I not made.* The little money he left to his family showed how true this was.

Knox's true legacy was the lasting spiritual, moral and indeed social changes he pioneered in his native Scotland to the benefit of many generations to come. There would soon be a school in every parish to help plant the Word of God in every heart.

BC

Footnote

1. *The History of the Reformation in Scotland*, 5 volumes, written between 1559 and 1566.

CHAPTER 8

The Reformation in England

"Lord! Open the King of England's eyes!" This fervent prayer of William Tyndale martyred on 6th October 1536 was heard in heaven (see chapter 2) and soon answered, but whether the mind of Henry VIII was ever truly enlightened to spiritual truths would be difficult to say.

The first Tudor king, Henry VII, won the crown when he defeated Richard III, sinister uncle of the princes in the Tower, and the last Plantagenet king, in battle at Bosworth Field in 1485. The victory effectively ended the Wars of the Roses and brought final triumph to the Lancastrians. The Tudors reigned from the late medieval period to early in the modern era. The focus of their foreign policy gradually moved away from retaining historic Continental possessions in France, to the beginnings of a global maritime challenge to Spain in the exploits of sailors and navigators like Martin Frobisher, Sir Francis Drake (who had time to play bowls before routing the Spanish Armada), Sir Walter Raleigh and other Elizabethan adventurers.

So there were significant changes in the sixteenth century but the greatest event of these times was neither political nor economic, it was spiritual. It was the Reformation. The differing responses of successive Tudor monarchs to the Reformation defined their reigns. Henry VIII's attitude to reform would be governed by convenience. Matrimonial, financial and political issues counted with him. Edward VI, though a youth, supported reform out of conviction, Mary suppressed reform with cruelty, and Elizabeth aimed to establish a reformed church by compromise. Through it all, behind the apparent authoritarian power of kings and queens, we recognise that "The king's heart is in the hand of the Lord, as the rivers of water: he turneth it whithersoever he will" (Prov 21.2).

The Path to Reformation

Henry VIII came to the throne of England in 1509, just eight years before Luther nailed his 95 Theses to the door of All Saints church in Wittenberg. Initially he strongly opposed Martin Luther's teachings and wrote a book in Latin *Assertio Septem Sacramentorum (Defence of the Seven Sacraments,* also known as the *Henrician Affirmation)* in which he defended papal supremacy and other doctrines. Pope Leo X rewarded Henry with the title *Defender of the Faith* in 1521. A later pope revoked the title when Henry broke with Rome and was excommunicated.[1] Henry had no problem with Romish dogma. His quarrel with the pope centred upon his determination to divorce his first wife Catherine of Aragon. Henry eventually lost patience with the protracted efforts to obtain Rome's approval of his divorce, and he and his advisers took matters into their own hands. Writs were issued against bishops and pressure exerted against the church, with the result that in May 1532 the English clergy largely acknowledged Henry as supreme governor of the Church of England. The king was now effectively his own pope, and his divorce from Catherine and marriage to Anne Boleyn swiftly followed.

In 1534 an Act of Parliament was passed which abolished Papal authority in the realm and put an end to payments of levies to Rome. This was not a true Reformation, but the appointments in 1533 of Thomas Cromwell as Chancellor, and Thomas Cranmer as Archbishop of Canterbury, paved the way for genuine reform in the longer term. Commissioners were appointed to visit Abbeys and Monasteries and to investigate their religious practices. Abuses were exposed leading to the *Suppression of Religious Houses Act* passed by Parliament in 1535. This Dissolution of the Monasteries led to substantial funds being appropriated by the Crown. Henry was always interested in the money! Yet he still firmly believed in transubstantiation, the veneration of saints and other Romish doctrines.

Henry's sixth and last marriage was to Katherine Parr. She brought a measure of stability and calm to the last years of Henry's life and judiciously sought to influence his mind towards evangelical truth. In the final hours of Henry's life on 28th January 1547 Cranmer was summoned to the king's bed chamber. Henry was still conscious but unable to speak so the archbishop held his hand and asked the king to give him a sign that he was trusting Jesus Christ for salvation. In response the grip on Cranmer's hand tightened slightly before Henry lapsed into unconsciousness and died. There had been little evidence in his life of a genuine conversion and one can only note, "The Lord knoweth them that are his".

The Pinnacle of Reformation

Edward VI (1537 – 1553) was only nine years old when he became king. He was the son of Jane Seymour, Henry's third queen. When he was born on 12th October 1537 London and the country had rejoiced. Just over a year had passed since William Tyndale's death and in remarkable ways the future Edward VI became the true answer to his prayer. Edward received a good education from his excellent tutor, the warm hearted Sir John Cheke, professor of Greek at Cambridge, and proved himself to be a highly intelligent pupil. Thomas Cranmer, a man of kindly disposition, was the king's godfather and a close spiritual bond existed between them. In a letter to Cranmer the king wrote "May your life be prolonged for many years, and may you continue to be a respected father to me by your godly and wholesome counsels. For I consider that godliness is to be desired and embraced by me above all things, since St Paul said, 'Godliness is profitable unto all things'".

The character of Edward's reign was presaged by an incident during the preparations for his coronation. When three swords representing his three kingdoms were brought to be carried in the procession, the king said "there was one yet wanting". When asked what that was he replied, "The Bible" and then added "that Book is the sword of the Spirit and is to be preferred before those. It ought in all right to govern us; without it we are nothing. He that rules without it is not to be called God's minister or a king".[2] Little wonder Cranmer in one of his sermons referred to Edward as England's Josiah. When only twelve years old the king wrote his *Treatise Against the Primacy of the Pope*. His quotations from the Epistle to the Romans reveal a sound understanding of Gospel truth. There is much evidence to show that Edward VI was a true and earnest Christian, a king whose eyes God indeed had opened!

The king's maternal uncle Edward Somerset was Lord Protector, effectively leader of the Privy Council, and with the support of Thomas Cranmer he pursued a steady course of reform. The *Act of Six Articles* of 1539 which had reasserted traditional Romish doctrines was abolished, and the first *Act of Uniformity* was passed in January1549. This Act established *The Book of Common Prayer* and required the use of a reformed liturgy. There was strong resistance to this in the north and south west of England, where the Reformation had made less progress.

The *Book of Common Prayer* was largely Cranmer's work assisted by Nicholas Ridley. Cranmer's beliefs had evolved over many years. He was not afraid to admit where he felt he had been wrong as he progressed towards a clearer understanding of Scripture. An example of this gradual progress can be seen in the nomination of John Hooper to the vacant bishopric of Gloucester. Hooper refused to take the customary oath of bishops at their consecration, or to wear the episcopal vestments. He objected to the oath as unscriptural, because it referred to the saints as well as to God, and to the vestments as a remnant of Popery which ought to be put away. This brought him into a controversy with Cranmer and Ridley. He was clearly ahead of them in scriptural understanding. Hooper's strong convictions delayed his consecration by a year until a compromise was reached. He agreed to wear his vestments on certain occasions, at his consecration, before the king, and in his own cathedral, and the king struck out the objectionable words from the Oath by his own hand. Hooper later suffered martyrdom at the stake in Gloucester.

In retrospect one's judgment of these men must be tempered by the circumstances in which they lived. To those who assert that the Reformers did their work badly, countenanced many abuses, and left many things imperfect and incomplete, J C Ryle wisely observed "In common fairness men should remember the numerous difficulties they had to contend with, and the mountains of rubbish they had to shovel away" and he added, "to my mind the wonder is not so much that they did so little, but rather that they succeeded in doing anything at all".

In 1552 Edward suffered an attack of measles and smallpox from which he never fully recovered. In the early months of 1553 he grew weaker and on 6th July, at only fifteen years of age, that brief but brightest reign in England's spiritual history was over. Shortly before the end he was heard to pray, "Lord have mercy upon me, take my spirit". His funeral service was held in Westminster Abbey on 8th August. The previous night his elder sister Mary had commanded that "the service should be said in her chapel in Latin as the custom was in Rome". Cranmer refused and insisted that as the King had been a zealous supporter of Reformation, the service should be in English and according to the existing English law.

Bishop Hooper said of Edward, *"He died young but lived long, if life be action."*

JB

Footnotes

1. The same title was granted to Henry and his successors by the English Parliament in 1544, and our coinage still bears the letters *FD,* sometimes *Fid Def,* abbreviating the Latin term *Fidei defensor.*

2. Miller's *Church History* Vol 3, page 1023

CHAPTER 9

The Persecution of Reformers –
the English Martyrs

Mary I (1516 -1558) was now queen. In the last months of Edward's life there had been intrigue to deprive her of the succession. An ill-advised and disastrous plot had been hatched to put Lady Jane Grey, a grandniece of Henry VIII on the throne. Jane, the nine day Queen of England, became an innocent tool of unscrupulous men, and she paid for their folly and ambition with her life. Most people felt that the throne belonged rightfully to Mary and she was acclaimed when she arrived in London. However the rejoicing at her accession was short lived. Her decision to marry Philip of Spain was deeply unpopular, and the beheading of sixteen year old Lady Jane on 12th February 1554 dismayed many.

It had been expected that Mary would insist upon her own right to celebrate Mass and continue the old practices, but she had a bigger agenda. It was to entirely reverse reform, return to 'the old religion', and bring the nation back under the authority of the See of Rome. This bigoted woman would stop at nothing to achieve her objective. She began by releasing all who had been imprisoned for their opposition to reform, and bishops of evangelical persuasion were dismissed to make way for men like Stephen Gardiner at Winchester, Edward Bonner at London and Dr Heath at Gloucester. Severe action against the reformers soon followed.

Latimer and Ridley at Oxford

The names Hugh Latimer and Nicholas Ridley remain inseparably linked in the annals of the period. Latimer was born about 1485. He studied at Cambridge and in 1510 was elected a Fellow of Clare Hall. In a sermon he recalled, "I was as obstinate a Papist as any was in England, insomuch that when I was made bachelor of divinity, my whole oration went against Philip Melanchthon and his opinions". Thomas Bilney a contemporary at Cambridge believed Latimer to be an honest man, and after the public attack on Melanchthon requested that he might make a confession of his own faith to Latimer in private. This courageous step resulted in Latimer's conversion. Bilney was later martyred, being burnt at the stake at Bishopsgate London in 1531.

Latimer commenced preaching in Cambridge University pulpits in a manner unheard of. He exhorted his hearers to search the Scriptures and enquire after the way of salvation. It was said of him that of a Saul God has made him a very Paul. In his zeal for the Gospel it was inevitable that many attacks were made against him. Surprisingly Henry VIII made him Bishop of Worcester in 1535, probably influenced by Thomas Cromwell and Thomas Cranmer. Preaching before a Convocation of the Clergy, Latimer said, "Lift up your heads brethren, and look about you with your eyes, and spy what things are to be reformed in the Church of England. Is it so hard, so great a matter, for you to see many abuses in the clergy and in the laity?" In 1539 he resigned his bishopric in protest at the passing of the semi-papist Act of the Six Articles.

He spent the last year of Henry's reign in prison but when Edward VI came to the throne he was immediately released. He preached before the king on the subject of marriage advising "to choose one that is of God, that is of the household of faith and such an one that the king can find in his heart to love, and to lead his life in pure and chaste espousage with". Latimer was one of the first to be apprehended after Mary's accession. He was committed to the Tower of London with Cranmer, Ridley and Bradford where for want of room all were in one chamber. These four carefully read and studied the New Testament together with great deliberation. From the Tower the three bishops were taken to Oxford in 1554 to prison and eventual matyrdom.

Nicholas Ridley was born about 1503 at Willimoteswick a hamlet in Northumberland near to the Scottish border. His early education was at a school in Newcastle-on-Tyne from which he went up to Pembroke College Cambridge where he became a distinguished scholar. Obscurity surrounds his conversion to the Protestant cause and it seems that light dawned upon him very gradually. In 1537 he became Chaplain to Archbishop Cranmer. It was not until 1545 that Ridley completely renounced the doctrine of the corporeal presence of Christ's body and blood in the sacrament. He rose rapidly from one office to another being nominated Bishop of Rochester in 1547, then of London in 1550 and in 1553 of Durham. This last appointment never took place as King Edward's death put a complete stop to Ridley's advancement.

As Bishop of London he had visited Lady Mary, as she then was, at her home to offer to preach before her. She disdainfully refused and concluded the conversation by saying "My lord, for your gentleness to come and see me I thank you, but for your offering to preach before me I thank you never a whit". After this she retained a particular aversion to Ridley. He was a gentle person and showed great courtesy and kindness to the old mother of Edward Bonner. Regrettably this was not reciprocated by Bonner after he was restored to the bishopric by Queen Mary. Like Latimer, Ridley was shamefully treated and persecuted when in prison but he manfully resisted every effort to induce him to recant.

The closing scenes of Latimer's and Ridley's lives took place close to Balliol College Oxford on 16th October 1555. Ridley arrived first and seeing Latimer he ran to him and kissed him saying, "Be of good heart brother, for God will either assuage the fury of the flames, or else strengthen us to abide it". They prayed together earnestly, and talked a little while, then had to listen to a sermon but were forbidden to answer anything that was said.

They were fastened back to back, to the same stake. Ridley's last words before the fire was lit were these: "Heavenly Father, I give Thee most hearty thanks that Thou hast called me to a profession of Thee even unto death. I beseech Thee, Lord God, have mercy on this realm of England, and deliver the same from all her enemies." Latimer's last words resound down the centuries, "Be of good comfort, Master Ridley, and play the man; we shall this day, by God's grace, light such a candle in England as I trust shall never be put out".

The faggots were lit and as the flames rose Ridley cried with a loud voice in Latin, "Into Thy hands, O Lord, I commend my spirit. Lord, receive my spirit". He then spoke the same words in English. Latimer cried vehemently on the other side of the stake, "Father of heaven, receive my soul". Latimer, an old man, soon died, but Ridley suffered long and painfully until the flames reached a vital part of his body, and he fell at Latimer's feet.

Cranmer at Oxford

In the life of Thomas Cranmer there had been arduous toil. At its end there was both tragedy and triumph. Mary never forgot that her mother's divorce had been brought about by Cranmer's advice and he was marked for destruction. Cranmer was tried but manfully resisted every argument. One of his judges stated, "We come to examine you, and methinks you examine us." Condemned as a heretic he was sentenced to be burned.

Severity had failed to force Cranmer to recant, but in the last month of his life came the tragedy. He was removed from prison and granted every indulgence in the home of the dean of Christ-church. This threw him off guard. Flattered and cajoled by subtle kindness, frightened at the prospect of so dreadful a death as burning, tempted and led away by the devil, Cranmer recanted and put his hand to a paper repudiating and renouncing the principles of the Reformation for which he had laboured so long. The news of Cranmer's recantation dismayed all true Protestants but it was not the end of the story. Had the Romanists then set Cranmer at liberty his name would have sunk in infamy, but they over reached themselves. Cranmer had been deceived. His persecutors were resolved to burn him even though he had recanted. The queen's revenge would only be satiated in his blood.

She ordered that a sermon should be preached shortly before his burning. On the appointed day 21st March 1556 the church was filled as Cranmer was brought in to a low stage to stand in torn dirty rags to thoroughly humiliate him. The preacher, Dr Reginald Pole, spoke of his atrocious crimes, encouraged him not to fear death and promised him that masses would be said for him in all the churches. Dr Pole then said that he had recanted from his heresy which he ascribed to the working of Almighty power and so that the people might be convinced of its reality asked the prisoner to give them a sign. Throughout the sermon Cranmer had wept bitter tears but now came his triumph. He fell upon his knees and prayed confessing his sins. Then rising he made a clear statement of his beliefs and spoke of the great thing that troubled his conscience "that is the setting abroad of a writing contrary to the truth, which now here I renounce and refuse, as things written with my hand contrary to the truth which I thought in my heart, and written for fear of death and to save my life, if it might be. And forasmuch as my hand hath offended, writing contrary to my heart, therefore my hand shall be first punished; for when I come to the fire it shall be first burned".

The congregation was amazed and indignant by this unexpected declaration and Dr Pole in anger cried "Lead the heretic away". John Foxe commented that Cranmer, like Samson completed a greater ruin upon his enemies in the hour of death, than he did in his life. The stake was ready at the same spot where Latimer and Ridley had been burnt. Reaching it Cranmer knelt for a short time in earnest devotion then arose and prepared for the fire. He was bound with an iron chain and the faggots were lit. As the flame ascended the martyr held out his right hand frequently exclaiming "this unworthy right hand". It was burnt to a cinder as he abode the burning with wonderful steadfastness. Thus in the fire, that good and noble man gave witness to his true beliefs.

Other Martyrs

It was not only prominent men who were made to suffer the fiendish cruelty of the Roman Church in those years. On 31st

January 1556 five persons were burnt, four of whom were women, one a widow. All were irreproachable in their lives, but they rejected absolution, indulgences, transubstantiation, and auricular confession. So they must die a cruel death! No less than 288 persons were burnt at the stake, an awful record. Just two days before the queen died five martyrs were burnt in one fire at Canterbury.

It was a mercy that the days of Mary's reign were shortened. The messenger who brought the news of her death to Elizabeth on 17th November 1558 found her reading her Greek New Testament. She was too overcome with emotion to speak for some moments, but then fell on her knees and exclaimed, "This is the Lord's doing, it is marvellous in our eyes".

These Marian martyrs, and the Scotsmen of Chapters 5 and 6 along with many others held their torches of testimony high, to lead the way into the light and liberty of the Gospel that has been enjoyed for so long throughout these British Isles.

JB

Footnote

Accounts of martyrdoms taken from *Foxe's Book of Martyrs* and from *Five English Reformers* by JC Ryle. In his book Ryle quotes extensively from Foxe.

CHAPTER 10

The King James Bible,
or The Authorised Version, 1611

1. *"To the Most High and Mighty Prince James ..."*

Thus begins the address of the *Epistle Dedicatory* penned on behalf of his fellow translators by Thomas Bilson. The King's majesty was humbly acknowledged in fulsome terms that James must have often enjoyed reading!

How did it come about that the Translation received "approbation and patronage from so learned and judicious a Prince", so that the name of King James remains well known wherever the English Bible is read? To answer that question one must consider events that led to the Union of the Crowns in 1603 when James VI of Scotland became James I of England, as well as the influence of James' childhood and training upon his attitude to religious questions.

Rulers of Scotland and England

The House of Stuart originated in the late mediaeval period, from the marriage of Marjorie, daughter of King Robert Bruce, hero of Bannockburn, to Robert Stewart. In 1503 James IV married Margaret Tudor, daughter of the English King Henry VII, forging the dynastic union which led to the Union of the Crowns one hundred years later.

The tragic history of Mary Queen of Scots, grand-daughter of James IV, is well known. She was sent for safety to France where she grew up and married Francis, heir to the French throne, who died after a brief reign. Mary returned to Scotland in 1561, arriving at Leith to the welcome of large crowds. She was a beautiful and courageous young woman but impulsive and injudicious.

After a belated start the Reformation had made great strides in Scotland, but Mary was a staunch Catholic. Her determination to celebrate Mass in the chapel at Holyrood on her first Sunday outraged the Lords of the Congregation and John Knox, who denounced the Mass in forthright terms as "a blasphemous idolatry". Her marriage to a cousin Henry Stewart, Lord Darnley, was rash and ill considered. He was a grandson (by her second marriage) of Margaret Tudor, Queen consort of James IV, and closer to the English throne than Mary. The marriage was brief and unhappy, but they had a son James born in June 1566. Darnley, a weak and petulant character, had made enemies, and in those violent times it was not long before he was murdered at Kirk o' Field close by Edinburgh. Events swiftly followed, leading to the forced abdication of Mary in favour of her infant son, and ultimately, after escape from prison on an island in Loch Leven, her flight to England.

Mary's presence in England perplexed Queen Elizabeth and her advisors. Now in her mid thirties Elizabeth remained unmarried and Mary was her presumptive heir. There was therefore a risk that Mary would become the focus of intrigue and rebellion for disaffected English Catholics desiring a Catholic monarch. The fear of plotting was heightened by the threat of invasion by Spain and this ultimately led to Mary's execution in 1587 after she was found to be implicated in a plot against Elizabeth. In twenty years of imprisonment she had never seen the Queen's face!

The young King James

Meanwhile Mary's son James was growing up in Scotland where he had to tread a rough road, learning how to survive amidst the violent and unruly ambitions of the Scottish nobility. Later he wrote of his youth, *"I was alane, without fader or moder, brither or sister, king of this realme, and heir apperand of England"*. He was brought up in Stirling Castle in the care of the Countess of Mar who showed some tenderness for him but he also experienced the stern discipline of his tutor George Buchanan, a disciple of John Knox and a scholar of great repute. Buchanan's regime was rigorous, but provided the boy king with a remarkable education in classical and modern languages with the result that no contemporary monarch was his intellectual equal. He was described when eighteen years of age as "an old young man".

The task of ruling Scotland must have seemed a daunting prospect, but James was subtle as well as intelligent, and began to advance his exercise of sovereignty in both political and religious affairs. The Scottish Reformation had produced a sternly Presbyterian Kirk whose leaders were not shy to tell the king exactly where he stood. In 1596 Andrew Melville had bluntly stated *"I mon tell yow, thair is twa Kings and twa Kingdomes in Scotland. Thair is Christ Jesus the King, and His Kingdome the Kirk, whase subject King James the Saxt is, and of whase Kingdome nocht a king nor a lord nor a heid, bot a member"*. Melville's theology was confused but his message was clear. He would brook no interference from the king in the government of the Kirk. This did not suit James who was developing his views on the Divine rights of Kings and the authority of the Crown over the General Assembly. He believed that an episcopal form of church government (as in England) provided a proper hierarchal structure at the head of which should be the Crown. James' theology too was flawed!

The Union of the Crowns

James had of course a strong interest in cultivating the friendship of Elizabeth and was careful to do nothing to jeopardise his hopes of succession. Though he was the strongest claimant, Elizabeth remained vague on the vital subject, and as she grew older it must have become a weary wait for James. At last however the old Queen died, and the news reached James in the Palace of Holyroodhouse on the evening of 26th March 1603. His succession to the English throne was now assured and before him lay the security, wealth and power of that throne.

James received a warm welcome in England and a great deal of flattery from parties anxious to promote their interests. There were many who regarded the Reformation in England as incomplete, and saw the new reign as an opportunity to rid the English Church of all vestiges of popery. A wide spectrum of views existed, from those who believed that each congregation should be independent and free from State authority, through supporters of a Presbyterian form of government and Puritans who objected to all ceremonial matters, to the bishops who resisted any change. To the bishops' horror, the Puritan suggestion for a conference to settle variances appealed to James, who considered himself a latter day Solomon and expert in theological and ecclesiastical matters.

The Hampton Court Conference

The Conference commenced on 12th January 1604 at Hampton Court. The King aimed for inclusiveness and harmony. His motto was *Beati Pacifico* – 'Blessed are the Peacemakers'. He presided over discussions rather cannily as one above party, and desiring unity. The bishops argued that the Elizabethan church had been as near the state of the primitive church as any in the world, and that there was no need of change. James disagreed, rebuking complacency - everything on earth was subject to decay and decline – nothing was perfect! The bishops were alarmed but they need not have worried. At heart James had no appetite for radical change. Only four representatives of the Puritans had been selected to attend and they quickly discovered, when raising matters relating to church government, that anything with a Presbyterian flavour was inimical to the King.

The Puritans however achieved a notable success when John Reynolds, Master of Corpus Christi Oxford, proposed a new English Translation of the Bible. The official version then used for public reading was the Bishop's Bible of 1568 - 72. It had many faults and was greatly disliked by the Puritans. Reynolds hoped for an English version much closer to the text of the Geneva Bible of 1560, translated by Calvinist Englishmen in Geneva. A defining feature of that Bible was its numerous and detailed marginal notes and references to which James objected, believing that "*some notes were very partial, untrue, seditious, and savouring too much of dangerous and traitorous conceits*". This revealed the King's obsessive fear of any challenge to royal authority. But he agreed with Reynolds that a new Bible was needed. The new version would not have Geneva style notes and interpretations alongside the text, and this probably disappointed Reynolds but its value would far exceed all that he could have imagined. The decision to authorise the translation which would bear the King's name was the major result of the Hampton Court Conference, and produced its lasting legacy.

James was an enigmatic character but perhaps he had "come to the kingdom for such a time as this". In retrospect we trace the providence of God behind the debates of a monarch, of prelates, of scholars, ensuring that His inspired, inerrant and infallible Word would be available in an English version of such dignity and beauty that for over four hundred years it has remained a worthy text for preaching and teaching.

2. *"Translated out of the Original Tongues: and with the Former Translations diligently compared and revised ..."*

Richard Bancroft, Bishop of London, soon to be Archbishop of Canterbury, believed "the king's business required haste". Thus he was exceedingly busy through the summer of 1604. Initially he had opposed John Reynolds' proposal for a new English translation, but royal approval made Bancroft diligent. It was His Majesty's pleasure to engage the most learned men, and letters were sent to such, urging their commitment to the project.

Bancroft was anti-Puritan, and in Elizabeth's reign had been relentless in his persecution of Separatists who believed each congregation to be a self sufficient Church. Many, driven from London, Lincolnshire, and Northamptonshire had fled to the Netherlands. They were the spiritual forebears of the Pilgrim Fathers, who fleeing intolerance and carrying their Geneva

Bibles, would sail to America in 1620 in the *Mayflower* to found the colony of Massachusetts. And yet Bancroft set about constructing a team of translators from a spectrum wide enough to embrace moderate Puritans. This is not altogether surprising, for the scholars of Jacobean England formed a relatively small community, and many who had studied together at the universities, remained friends though opposed in their beliefs.

King James was active with Bancroft in formulating rules to be observed by the six Companies of translators, each responsible for a prescribed part of Holy Scripture. Each Company had eight members giving a total of forty-eight translators. Over the period a number died and were replaced, so that over fifty contributed. The translators were diverse in their ecclesiastical views, but their contributions melded to produce a remarkable result. Two reasons for this may be suggested. First, all believed Scripture to be divinely inspired, making all conscious of their great responsibility. Second, the Company structure and rules fostered a spirit of co-operation.

The **First Westminster Company** was to translate from Genesis to II Kings. Its director was Lancelot Andrewes, Dean of Westminster, and a protagonist for ceremonial in the Church. He was renowned for his eloquence in an age of great preaching, being able to speak for an hour to enraptured congregations on the multiple significances of single words. The **First Cambridge Company** was given I Chronicles to Song of Songs. Laurence Chaderton, the leading Puritan at Cambridge and first Master of Emmanuel College, was its outstanding member. The college chapel was plainly furnished - a pulpit, a plain table and wooden benches. There were no surplices or gowns, and no kneeling for the sacrament. The bread and wine were passed from hand to hand by those sitting around the table. Chaderton, a man greatly loved and respected, lived to be over 100 years old. To the **First Oxford Company** was assigned the remainder of the Old Testament – Isaiah to Malachi. John Reynolds, Master of Corpus Christi was a leading member but died in 1607. Miles Smith, a strict Calvinist was another member. He kept no books in his library he had not read, and it was said of him, "he was covetous of nothing but books".

The **Second Cambridge Company** had responsibility for the Apocrypha (the inter testament books). John Bois was a member who also assisted members of other Companies. John's father William Bois had been delivered from the yoke of Rome while studying at Trinity College, Cambridge in the early 1550s. During the Marian persecutions, like many others he fled to Hadleigh in Suffolk. Foxe's Book of Martyrs, records that Hadleigh then "seemed rather an university of the learned than a town of labouring people". John Bois was of high intellectual ability and a brilliant Greek student at Cambridge. The Gospels, Acts of the Apostles and Revelation were given to the **Second Oxford Company** of which George Abbot, a future Archbishop of Canterbury, and Sir Henry Savile were members. Abbot's parents had "embraced the truth of the Gospel in King Edward's reign and were persecuted for it in Queen Mary's reign". Abbot, a strong Calvinist, supported the idea of bishops, but in what he termed "a superintending pastorate". Savile a brilliant scholar, mathematician and classicist was the only translator who had not taken "holy orders". The **Second Westminster Company** translated all of the New Testament Epistles. Its Director was William Barlow, Dean of Chester and later Bishop of London. Barlow, an obsequious man, wrote the official record of the Hampton Court Conference.

Instructions to the Translators

A copy of the instructions to the Translators is preserved in the University Library in Cambridge. The first rules addressed style and content, e.g., "*The Bishop's Bible to be followed, and as little altered as the Truth of the Original will permit*". The English translations to be consulted were Tyndale's, Matthew's, Coverdale's, Geneva. The latter was generally acknowledged as being superior to the Bishop's Bible from which comparatively little phraseology was actually used. The rule that "*The old ecclesiastical words to be kept viz. as the word Church not to be translated Congregation & etc.*" is apparent in the epistles.

William Tyndale had translated *ecclesia* as congregation. The words oversight and overseer would later be used in 1 Timothy 3.1, 2, but "churches" and "bishops" prevailed in 1611. No ground was given, either to Presbyterians or Separatists!

Later rules aimed for cohesion in the Translation, e.g., *"every man of each company was to take the same chapters and having translated or amended them severally by himself; all to meet together confer and agree what shall stand"*, and *"as one company hath despatched a book they shall send it to the rest to be considered seriously and judiciously; for His Majesty is very careful of this point"*. Finally *"if any company on review of the books so sent really doubt, or differ on any place, to send them word thereof, to note the place, and give their reasons to which if they consent not the difference was to be compounded at the general meeting of the chief persons of each company at the end of the work."*

In 1689 the historian John Seldon wrote about meetings of the final committee: *"The Translators in King James's time took an excellent way. That part of the Bible was given to him who was most excellent in such a tongue... and then they met together, and one read the translation, the rest holding in their hands some Bible, either of the learned tongues, or French, Spanish, Italian etc. If they found any fault they spoke; if not he read on".* This reading aloud as part of the checking process contributed to the excellent rhythmic readability of the Authorised Version.

Source Greek Text

The *Textus Receptus* or Received Text was used in translating the New Testament. This Greek text was largely the work of Erasmus (d. 1536) but the term Received Text was not used until 1633 when an edition of Erasmus's Greek New Testament, with a little revision by Stephanus, was reprinted. This text was used for almost all New Testament translation work until the 1880s. Much scholarship has been devoted to genuine textual criticism as ancient manuscripts have since been discovered, with a view to establishing a more accurate text. Many learned men still express their confidence in the Received Text as being fundamentally reliable.

So the materials available to the Translators were the texts of the ancient languages, and the work of former translators. These included the noble and heroic Tyndale martyred in 1536 because he defied the Pope and the Church's hierarchy to make the Bible accessible to English readers. Tyndale's achievements in translation were magnificent, both in their spiritual and literary value. Seventy-five years after his death, his work gave over eighty per cent of the New Testament and over seventy per cent of the Old in the KJV. The rhythms, vocabulary and cadences of the KJV and its dominance as an English Bible clearly owe much to Tyndale as we noted in Chapter 2.

3. **"As that we have great hopes that the Church of England shall reap good fruit thereby ..."**

In these terms the Translators expressed their hopes in The Epistle Dedicatory, and over four hundred years later, good fruit continues to be reaped in a field wider than those worthy men could ever have imagined.

The success of the translation was not immediate as many Puritans clung to their Geneva Bibles, replete with marginal notes and references, but in time the Authorised Version, as it came to be known, captured the affection of English speaking people word wide. On a historical scale the sheer longevity of the AV is a phenomenon without parallel.[1]

Tyndale's Influence

Much credit is due to Tyndale who had combined the requisites for successful translation, i.e., technical skill and fluency in the original tongues, with sensitivity to the idiom of the language of the translation. Tyndale was outstanding in matching varieties of English to the differences in Hebrew, and one of the first to appreciate the Hebrew influence on New Testament Greek.[1] He translated with clarity and accuracy using simple English syntax.

The reading of his text gave impetus to the development of

the English language. It has been observed "without Tyndale no Shakespeare", and one could add, no Donne, Johnson or Spenser. Through the decades following Tyndale's martyrdom English prose and poetry gained a new vibrancy, and it was in that bright spring-time of English literature that King James's translators applied themselves to their task. Their great achievement was to bring a Jacobean richness of beauty and dignity to their revision, expressing the extraordinary power and flexibility of the English language. The result has been to give us the Bible in language of musicality and rhythm eminently suited for public reading.

Modern Versions

The 20th century witnessed a plethora of modern versions, many of which swiftly sank into well-deserved obscurity, while the AV sails on majestically, still the best selling book in the world. A serious post war endeavour was the New English Bible proposed in 1946. The Joint Committee overseeing that work met in the Jerusalem Chamber of Westminster Abbey, the place where Lancelot Andrewes and his Company had gathered long before. Perhaps they hoped for inspiration!

But for example, contrast the banality of the NEB rendering of John 21.4-6:

> Morning came and there stood Jesus on the beach......
> He called out to them "Friends, have you caught anything?" They answered "No". He said, "Shoot the net to starboard, and you will make a catch."

with the atmospheric AV narrative:

> But when morning was now come, Jesus stood on the shore...Then Jesus saith unto them, "Children, have ye any meat?" They answered him, "No". And he said unto them, "Cast the net on the right side of the ship, and ye shall find."

TS Elliot wrote that the NEB "astonishes in its combination of the vulgar, the trivial, and the pedantic". Attempts in modern versions to translate in language claimed to be more easily understood by a modern reader, have usually resulted in a flattening of the tone, in a sense that the sublime has been sacrificed for the prosaic, leaving one feeling the loss of something "so touching in its majesty".[2] Furthermore, serious doctrinal questions have arisen regarding verses and passages in certain modern versions, that have been found to express not always fully, and sometimes not faithfully or completely, the truth contained in the original. The tendency to use modern versions for public reading has been regrettable. And yet the cadences of the Authorised Version may still be heard on great occasions, as if there lingers, amidst the rush for mediocrity, a desire for old certainties and things of beauty. Some argue that its language is archaic and incomprehensible to young people, and thus we need to use a version in the language of our time. But one then questions whether the language of our time is really capable of conveying the sublime truths of the Word of God.

Allowing for the current failings of State education, it remains true that most people are well able to understand a reading from the AV. Its language is timeless, and memorable phrases remain in the national consciousness. People express what they regard as proverbial wisdom, not realising they are quoting scripture. *"Escaped with the skin of my teeth"* (Job 19.20) is one example. *"Am I my brother's keeper?"* (Gen 4.9) is another. Winston Churchill could quote scripture to good effect as when in a wartime speech he declared of the Nazis *"They have sown the wind, and they shall reap the whirlwind"* (Hos 8.7).

JN Darby was an accomplished linguist who translated the Bible into both French and English. In the Preface to his New Testament published in 1871 he made the following interesting observation. "Those who make a version for public use must of course adapt their course to the public. Such has not been my object or thought, but to give to the student of scripture, who cannot read the original, as close a translation as possible." Obviously Darby intended his translation to be used for private study rather than for public reading. He commented on the

Authorised Version: "Its value and beauty are known, and I need not dilate upon. I have lived upon it, though of course studying the Greek myself".

A Perfect Translation?

Some venerate the Authorised Version to the extent that they claim inspiration for the translators! But only the writers of the original text were inspired. Paul makes this clear in 2 Timothy 3.16: "All scripture is given by inspiration of God". Peter referring to the Old Testament wrote that "holy men of God spake as they were moved by the Holy Ghost" (2 Pet 1.21). In the same letter, the epistles of Paul are put on a level with "the other scriptures" (3.15, 16). A thoughtful reader will see that these verses refer to the original documents as being inerrant and authoritative scripture.

Inspiration cannot be claimed for the process of translation. That process will depend upon the skill and integrity of the translator(s), to ensure accuracy as far as humanly possible, and upon divine help and blessing in their work. It will be appreciated that original documents had ceased to exist long before 1611. The Translators, like others, used Hebrew and Greek texts derived from manuscripts which themselves were copies, and in which there may have been some minor errors.

It would take a bold person to assert that the AV is perfect. Perhaps there is no such a thing as the perfect translation. The AV does have inaccurate readings at various points. A well known example is at Hebrews 2.17 where the Greek *hilaskomai* which means 'to propitiate', was translated "*to make reconciliation for the sins of the people*", although in 1 John 2.2 and 4.10 the noun form of the word was translated correctly as 'propitiation'. At Hebrews 2.17 JND gives "*to make propitiation for the sins of the people*", which is more satisfactory and accurate.

Conclusion

Notwithstanding such matters, the AV is an excellent and reliable English Bible. Three reasons may be adduced to support that assertion:

1. the providence of God overruling in a work which history has shown to be of global importance;

2. the basic reliability of the Hebrew and Greek texts used;

3. the translation coinciding with a flowering both of language and of literary genius.

Miles Smith, Bishop of Gloucester and one of the First Oxford Company wrote the lengthy Preface to the King James Bible entitled *The Translators to the Reader*. It includes these memorable words:

> *Translation it is that openeth the window, to let in the light; that breaketh the shell, that we may eat the kernel; that putteth aside the curtain, that we may look into the most Holy Place; that removeth the covering of the well, that we may come by the water.*

Successive generations of Torchbearers of the Truth have drawn from that well, and multitudes have been refreshed.

JB

Footnotes

1. *The Bible in English* by David Daniel, published by Yale University Press

2. From *Upon Westminster Bridge* by William Wordsworth

CHAPTER 11

Samuel Rutherford (1600 – 1661)

"In Immanuel's Land"

The well loved hymn *Immanuel's Land* which is in most of our hymnbooks has helped to perpetuate the name of Samuel Rutherford. It was not actually written by Rutherford but is taken from a long poem which Anne Ross Cousin wrote in 1856. After a lifetime's study of his life and letters she wrote the nineteen verses which skilfully evoke Rutherford's own words and feelings.[1] A constant theme of those letters is the sweetness of Christ and the emptiness of this passing world. They show him to be one of the most godly men Scotland has known, a beacon light in the darkness of the seventeenth century. It shines to this day.

Rutherford lived just before the terrible "killing times" of the Scottish Covenanter movement. His life bridges the sixteenth century Reformation and the later evangelical revivals. The torch of truth which he held and passed on even to us today was based upon his deep personal knowledge of Christ born out of long hours of communion and intimacy with Him. His devotion to Christ in those turbulent years led to his imprisonment in mid career, and would have led to his martyrdom later if his call to *Immanuel's Land* had not forestalled his accusers' plot to send him to his execution as they sent others.[2]

Early Life

Samuel Rutherford was born in a village near Jedburgh in the Scottish Borders, one of three sons of a prosperous farmer. He sent him to the University of Edinburgh where in 1621 he obtained his MA, two years later being appointed professor of Latin language and literature. But in 1626 he resigned to begin studying theology, having become "seriously religious".

What had happened was that, aged about twenty-four, he was converted and afterwards wrote: "He hath fettered me with His love...and left me a chained man," and explained: "Oh, but Christ hath a saving eye! Salvation is in His eyelids! When He first looked on me, I was saved." He regretted not having sought the Lord sooner, writing: "Like a fool, as I was, I suffered my sun to be high in the heaven, and near afternoon, before ever I took the gate by the end." He warned that none should "loiter on the broad road too long, trifling at the gate".

Anwoth by the Solway

In 1627 he accepted an invitation from Lord Kenmure of Cardoness Castle in Kirkcudbrightshire to come to preach in the new parish of Anwoth where his ministry would last for nine years. Busy and fruitful they would be. Visiting the many scattered hamlets in this rural parish was a task in itself. He often rose at 3am for worship, prayer and communion with Christ. One wrote, "He seemed to be always praying, always preaching, always visiting the sick, always catechising, always writing or studying." His great burden was for souls and he wrote: "If the Lord furnish not new timber from Lebanon to build the house, the work will cease." He said that he would "be glad to know of one soul to be my crown and rejoicing in the day of Christ". He often paced up and down the path outside his house pleading for souls and for divine help to reach them. This path became known as Rutherford's Walk.

He had many trials and discouragements. His two children died in infancy and then in 1629 his wife Eupham contracted a lingering disease from which she died over a year later. He wrote, "My wife is so sore tormented night and day, that I have wondered why the Lord tarrieth so long. It is hard to keep sight of God in a storm." Just after this he developed a fever himself which lasted for thirteen weeks and he was hardly able to preach.

Imprisonment

His greatest trial came when Thomas Sydserff became Bishop of Galloway. He was an arrogant supporter of Archbishop William Laud, the right-hand man of King Charles I who wanted to reintroduce the episcopacy and its litany into Scottish churches. Rutherford published a *Treatise against Arminianism* which exposed the doctrinal errors of Laud. As a consequence of this, Rutherford was summoned to an ecclesiastical court in Wigtown, then in Edinburgh. He was forbidden to preach in Scotland and was banished to Aberdeen where he would spend the next two years under house arrest at 44 Upper Kirkgate.

His immediate reaction to this sentence was quiet resignation and even joy, but as time wore on he seriously missed the privilege of preaching the Word of God and serving his Anwoth flock. He called these his "dumb Sabbaths". The devil suggested to him that God had cast him off, that he was a spiritual failure. But eventually he was able to call Aberdeen his garden of delights, and in "his sea-beat prison" his Lord and he "held tryst". He enjoyed so much of the love of God in Christ that he could write: "Christ and His cross are sweet company, and a blessed couple. My prison is my palace, my sorrow is with child of joy, my losses are rich losses, my pain easy pain." On the other hand he wrote: "I find the townsmen cold, general, and dry in their kindness. Many think me a strange man, and my cause not good."

Like another "prisoner of Jesus Christ" his confinement benefited many. It was his main letter-writing period – altogether 365 letters have been preserved.[3] Although the old style of writing makes them difficult to read at times, they are a soul tonic and a challenge to the lesser godliness of today.

To St Andrews

In 1638 the National Covenant was signed in Edinburgh, granting freedom to Nonconformist churches. Rutherford discharged himself from exile and returned to Anwoth to the great joy of his waiting people. But less than a year later he was asked to take the influential position of Professor of Divinity at St Mary's College, St Andrews. Reluctantly he agreed, leaving Anwoth for the second and last time.

St Andrews University had by then acquired a bad reputation: "the very nursery of all superstition in worship and error in doctrine and the sink of all profanity in conversation among the students". But Rutherford transformed the College to produce many godly men who would go to preach the Gospel in Scotland. Although invited to better posts he remained there, becoming Principal of the College in 1647. For four years before that he was absent in London, involved in formulating the *The Westminster Confession of Faith*. He continued to write letters, books and pamphlets. After ten years of widowhood he married Jean McMath. They had seven children of whom only one, Agnes, survived. She was eleven years old when he died.

In 1660, Oliver Cromwell's death removed several years' restraint on Roman Catholicism in Scotland. Charles II was restored to the throne and began to reverse the work of the Reformation. Rutherford was now a marked man, particularly for his book *Lex Rex* written in 1644, which opposed the absolute powers of the monarchy. It was publicly burned in Edinburgh and St Andrews.

He was deprived of all his offices and summonsed to appear before the king on a charge of treason. When the summons document reached him, he was a very sick man. Taking it in his hands, his famous reply was, "Tell them that I have a summons already from a superior Judge and judicatory and I behove to answer my first summons. Ere your day arrives I shall be where few kings and great men come."

Among his last words to his friends were, "My Lord and Master is the chief of ten thousand, none is comparable to Him in heaven or earth. Dear brethren, do all for Him; pray for Christ, preach for Christ, feed the flock committed to your charge for Christ, do all for Christ; beware of men-pleasing - there is too much of it amongst us." Another asked him, "What think ye now of Christ?" He answered, "I shall live and adore Him. Glory!

glory to my Creator and my Redeemer for ever! Glory shines in Immanuel's land."

In the afternoon of 28th March 1661 he was heard to say, "Oh! that all my brethren in the land may know what a Master I have served, and what peace I have this day. I shall sleep in Christ, and when I awake I shall be satisfied with His likeness. This night shall close the door, and put my anchor within the veil. Oh! for arms to embrace Him! Oh! for a well-tuned harp!"

By 5am the next morning he had entered into it all.[4]

BC

Footnotes

1. *"The sands of time are sinking ..."* Full poem and original tune *Rutherford* in www. cyberhymnal.org

2. In May and June of 1661, two of Rutherford's friends and colleagues, the Marquis of Argyll and James Guthrie, were publicly executed, and a third, Archibald Johnstone, escaped this fate by fleeing to the continent.

3. *Letters of Samuel Rutherford* , Andrew Bonar 1848, 1863 & 1891. Abridged version with 69 letters published by Banner of Truth Trust, Edinburgh, 1973.

4. His gravestone and its poetic epitaph are worth seeing in St Andrews old cemetery behind the ruined cathedral.

CHAPTER 12

John Bunyan (1628 -1688)

"The Pilgrim's Progress"

John Bunyan's torch has shone brightly far and wide. Apart from the Bible itself, no book has been so influential in bringing the gospel to so many people in so many countries as his *Pilgrim's Progress*. It was once the most widely read and translated book in the English language. Since its publication in 1678 it has never been out of print. It has been translated into over 200 languages. It was the first book foreign missionaries used alongside the Bible. Once read, who can forget the lines,

> *Blest cross! Blest sepulchre! Blessed rather be*
> *The Man who there was put to shame for me?*

Its full original title is *The Pilgrim's Progress From This World to That Which Is to Come Delivered Under the Similitude of a Dream*. It is an extended allegory set in 17th century England with locations which match some parts of Bedfordshire, but the story is so graphic and realistic, the language so evocative and resonating that it has long outlived its times. Some more modern renderings have been made through the centuries and it has been simplified into children's versions, but none is as good as the original.

It was once a standard textbook in British schools, and in great English literature it has been ranked by experts alongside John Milton's *Paradise Lost* and Geoffrey Chaucer's *Canterbury Tales*. By 1692, four years after the author's death, publisher Charles Doe estimated that 100,000 copies had been printed in

England. By 1938, 250 years after Bunyan's death, more than 1,300 editions of the book had been printed.

What makes this all the more remarkable is that the author had very little formal education, was a tinker to trade, and wrote the book while he was in jail. And this author also produced over forty other books and pamphlets, notably *Grace Abounding* which is the story of the long road to his own conversion, and *The Holy War,* another allegory which tells of the recovery of the Town of Mansoul from Diabolus by Prince Emmanuel. His quaint but stirring hymn *Who would true valour see ...* comes from the later pages of *Pilgrim's Progress*.

His Background

John Bunyan was born in November 1628 at Elstow, about a mile from Bedford. His father Thomas Bunyan was a tinker, making and mending pots and kettles, and his mother was Margaret Bentley. Their family life was a struggle with poverty, but young John later wrote, "It pleased God to put it into their hearts to put me to school, to learn me both to read and write." He also tells us that in his early years he was "filled with all unrighteousness", and that he indulged in much "cursing, swearing, lying, and blaspheming the holy name of God". At the same time, he was "greatly afflicted and troubled with the thoughts of the fearful torments of hell-fire".

When he was sixteen, his mother died, and also his sister Margaret. His father married again soon afterwards, and a step-brother, Charles was born. John left home to spend the next three years as a soldier in the parliamentary army during the English civil war. An incident from that time made him think seriously about eternity: one night a fellow soldier who had just taken his place on sentry duty was killed by a musket bullet.

After leaving the army he took up his tinker's trade and in 1650 he got married to a pious woman called Mary. Of his wife he writes, "This woman and I, though we came together as poor as poor might be (not having so much household stuff as a dish or a spoon betwixt us both), yet this she had for her part, *The*

Plain Man's Pathway to Heaven and *The Practice of Piety."* With these books and the help of his wife he recovered his almost lost ability to read. He also entered a period of deep spiritual struggle which he records in his *Grace Abounding to the Chief of Sinners* (1666), and is the background to the earlier part of *Pilgrim's Progress.*

From this marriage they had three daughters and two sons. Their first daughter Mary was blind and John always showed a deep care for her until she died in 1680. In 1658, after the birth of Thomas, his wife Mary died. A year later he married Elizabeth – they had a daughter, and then a son in 1672. During these years John Bunyan became a changed man, a persecuted follower of Christ, and a prolific writer who would leave behind him such a lasting spiritual legacy.

His Conversion

His spiritual struggles centred around conviction of sin and fear of divine displeasure and punishment. He feared that he had committed the unpardonable sin. A sermon denouncing labour and sports on the Lord's Day specially moved him. Some time later while passing through the streets of Bedford, he tells us that he heard "three or four poor women" sitting at a door "talking about the new birth, the work of God in their hearts, and the way by which they were convinced of their miserable state by nature. They told how God had visited their souls with His love in Christ Jesus."

He began to seek the Lord and he read the Scriptures more earnestly. Sometimes he would find encouragement to trust Christ, frequently he would relapse into despair, seeking and not finding what he looked for. Later he recounts, "As I was passing into the field ... fearing yet that all was not right, suddenly this sentence fell upon my soul, 'Thy righteousness is in heaven ...' for my righteousness was Jesus Christ Himself, the same yesterday, today, and forever. Now did my chains fall off ... my temptations also fled away. Now I went home rejoicing for the grace and love of God."

John Bunyan found a spiritual home in an independent congregation in Bedford led by John Gifford who baptized him (by immersion) in 1655. He continued to work as a tinker, but he soon became recognized by his friends as a gifted preacher. He preached with great fervour and power in towns and villages around. But with no "legal license" to preach he was indicted in 1658. However, no record of any sentence exists and he just continued preaching.

Bedford Jail

In 1660 Charles II was restored to the monarchy and there was a clampdown on Nonconformists. A Bedford justice learned that Bunyan was to preach near the village of Lower Samsall and issued a warrant for his arrest. In the middle of the sermon a constable entered and arrested him and put him into Bedford Jail to await the next Quarter Sessions. He was charged with "being a common upholder of several unlawful meetings and conventicles to the great disturbance and distraction of the good subjects of this kingdom". The sentence was three more months in jail, and if then he "should not submit to go to church and leave off preaching" he should be "banished the realm". If found in the country after that, he should hang. This sentence was not carried through, but Bunyan was left in Bedford jail for twelve years. That was when many of his books were written. He supported his family by making "long tagged laces" and he had periods of relative freedom when his jailers allowed him out to preach. Inside he also preached regularly to around fifty prisoners at a time.

In 1672 the king suspended all the statutes against Nonconformists and Bunyan received royal authority to preach in the Bedford church where his congregation soon numbered 4,000. He also established over thirty new congregations nearby. His reputation extended as far as London, where great crowds gathered to hear him and he became chaplain to the Lord Mayor.

This period of freedom was short lived, however, for in 1675 many licenses to preach were withdrawn and soon a warrant was issued for the arrest of Bunyan on the charge of "having preached to or teached at a Conventicle meeting or assembly under colour or pretense of exercise of religion in other manner than according to the Liturgie or Practice of the Church of England". He was imprisoned this time for six months, probably in the one-room jail on the bridge over the River Ouse and it is here that most of *Pilgrim's Progress* was written. Once published it was so popular that Bunyan's later years became very influential, with his services called upon all over England, though not entirely free from the danger of ecclesiastical interference.

To "the Celestial City"

His life ended suddenly at the age of sixty. His extensive writing and publishing work were taking their toll on his health. In the summer of 1688 he was asked to go to Reading to resolve a dispute between a father and his son. On the way back to London he was soaked in a rainstorm and developed pneumonia. He died ten days later at the house of his friend, John Strudwick in Holborn Bridge on 31st August. He was buried at Bunhill Fields cemetery, London where his gravestone may still be seen.

So this pilgrim reached the Celestial City - *"he passed over, and all the trumpets sounded for him on the other side".*

BC

CHAPTER 13

John Owen (1616 – 1683)

It was bitterly cold in London on 30th January 1649 yet a huge throng was gathered in Whitehall as King Charles I walked through an open window of the Banqueting House and stepped onto a platform to meet his death. He stood perfectly composed, warmly clad lest he should shiver and be thought to be afraid. After delivering a short speech he lay down to place his head upon the block. When the King had stretched out his hands the axe fell, cutting through his neck with a single blow. It is said that a groan spread through the crowd as the executioner lifted up the severed head. The words of one observer have become famous: "such a groan by the thousands then present, as I never heard before and I desire I may never hear again". Kings of England, and of Scotland had fallen in battle or had been assassinated, but none before had been tried for treason, found guilty and executed. It was a momentous day.

The Puritans

The day following a young Puritan minister preached before the English Parliament. He was John Owen and in his sermon he made no reference to the events of the previous day. There was no drama; rather a sober reminder of the duties of the Members and a call for humility and steadfastness. Owen's life intertwined with the lives of great men, labouring in a critical age of great events, yet he made his mark for God. His gifts became widely recognised by his contemporaries and many since have considered him to be the greatest of Puritan theologians. The term 'Puritan' is often used in a pejorative sense, so it should be understood that mainstream Puritans in the 16th and 17th centuries were orthodox Christians who wished to see the worship and government of the Church of England conforming more completely to the scriptural pattern. Their convictions were similar to those of John Hooper the martyred Bishop of Gloucester (see Chapter 8).

Owen's family and education

The Owen family was of Welsh extraction but lived at Stradham in Oxfordshire where John was born in 1616. He had an older brother William who also became a minister and two younger brothers, Henry and Philemon who both served in the army. Philemon was killed in Ireland in 1649. John went up to Queen's College Oxford when only 12 years old. His classical education included Hebrew, Greek, Latin, logic and philosophy. He was an unusually diligent and disciplined student often allowing himself only four hours sleep. After graduating M A in 1635, he began the seven year Bachelor of Divinity degree course, but conditions at that time at Oxford University were not favourable to men of Puritan persuasion and Owen left after only two further years.

William Laud, Archbishop of Canterbury since 1633, was reaching the height of his power and influence. He had been appointed university chancellor in 1630 and had reintroduced high liturgy to the university chapel services. Such forms of ceremony and liturgy, and his Arminian beliefs were inimical to Puritan thought. Laud was intolerant of opposition and tried to enforce conformity to his 'reforms'. He made a major mistake by insisting upon conformity in Scotland (affecting Samuel Rutherford – see Chapter 11). The Scots were already affronted by the King's efforts to impose Episcopalian rule and the use of a new Prayer Book led to the famous incident on 23rd July 1637 when Jenny Geddes flung her stool down the nave of St Giles Kirk in Edinburgh. The Prayer Book riots that followed became the precursor to drafting the *National Covenant* signed by thousands of Scots. This was a major step in the inexorable descent to the outbreak of Civil War in 1642.[1]

Conversion and convictions during the Civil War

1642 was also eventful in the life of John Owen. After leaving Oxford he had found employment as a private tutor and chaplain until he lost his place because of his sympathy for the Parliamentary cause. Thus in 1642 he came to London. One Sunday he went to hear Edmund Calamy a well-known Presbyterian minister. Calamy was unable to preach however Owen remained to hear Calamy's substitute speaking on the words of Christ following the calming of the storm, "Why are ye fearful, O ye of little faith?" As he listened he was brought into a new sense of peace and assurance which would characterise his life and ministry. Later in the year his first publication *A Display of Arminianism* appeared. It was the beginning of an extraordinary literary output.

In 1643 he became minister at Fordham in Essex. While there he married Mary Rooke who bore him eleven children only one of whom survived into adulthood. In 1646 he was appointed to serve at St Peter's, Coggeshall also in Essex. At this time, when only 30 years old, he preached for the first time to the Members of Parliament on the contentious subject of Church Government. He had held Presbyterian views but now moved towards an independent congregational position. The second civil war began in 1648 and in the summer of that year an army under the command of the successful General Sir Thomas Fairfax was besieging the Royalists in Colchester. It has been said that civil wars are the most cruel and brutal of wars, and in this lengthy and increasingly ferocious siege fearful atrocities were perpetrated. Owen became a friend of Fairfax and when he was invited to address the army he urged the officers and men against religious persecution. Tolerant and moderate men like Owen were much needed at such a time.

When Oliver Cromwell with an army crossed to Ireland in 1649 to subdue rebellion, Owen accompanied him as his chaplain. This campaign is remembered chiefly because of the siege of Drogheda. Cromwell has been vilified for the carnage and killing that ensued upon the breaching of the walls, and the storming of the city. Some historians now concede that the victims were neither Irish Catholics nor unarmed civilians, rather soldiers of the mainly Protestant Royalist defending army. Cromwell certainly made an example of them to deter further rebellion. Owen's perspective was different. His knowledge of what had happened stirred him to eloquence when he preached before Parliament after his return. He said, "How is it that Jesus Christ is in Ireland only as a lion staining all his garments with the blood of his enemies; and none to hold him out as a lamb sprinkled with his own blood to his friends?" He continued, "I would that there were for the present one gospel preacher for every walled town in the English possessions in Ireland. The land mourneth, and the people perish for want of knowledge. The tears and cries of the inhabitants of Dublin after the manifestations of Christ are ever in my view." In this he showed himself to be not the servant of men but of God. After being with Cromwell in Scotland in 1650 Owen returned to Coggeshall and resumed his pastoral duties.

Academic life during the Protectorate

Puritan influence reached its high watermark during the Commonwealth and Protectorate when many Puritans occupied responsible posts. John Owen was made Dean of Christ Church Oxford in 1651, and in the following year Cromwell appointed him vice-chancellor of the university. Oxford had been badly affected by the civil war when the military had commandeered many buildings and five of the colleges were deserted. Owen was an able administrator and he re-invigorated the university. He preached regularly in his college and in St Mary's Church. One of Owen's books *On the Mortification of Sin* is an edited collection of sermons preached to the students during this period. He also served as a 'Trier', that is he was responsible for assessing fitness for Gospel ministry. In that capacity he acted with kindness and moderation. Though a supporter of Cromwell, Owen was troubled by the proposal in 1657 that he should become king. Owen personally favoured a republic. In the event Cromwell declined the offer of the throne.

After the Restoration

1660 was a year of restoration, of the monarch and of Episcopalian hierarchy - not only a king again but bishops too! The Restoration parliament passed Acts collectively known as the Clarendon Code. The 1662 Act of Uniformity adversely affected the spirituality of the Church of England. Over 2,000 of its clergy were forced to resign because they could not in good conscience comply with the Act which enforced the use of the Book of Common Prayer, and restored Episcopal ordination which had been abolished during the Protectorate. Owen refused to conform and this brought his service at Oxford University to an end. In 1663 he was invited to become pastor at the First Congregational Church in Boston, Massachusetts but refused the offer. He preferred to remain in England, and was content to minister to a small independent congregation. Owen and others like him must have been deeply grieved, not by their loss of position and influence, but by the awful licentiousness of the Stuart Court and the general reaction of the populace against puritan morality.

Owen's life became relatively secluded, but his high reputation gave him opportunities to help other Independents or Dissenters. He was a friend of John Bunyan (Chapter 12) and assisted arrangements for the publication of *The Pilgrim's Progress*. Through his remaining years Owen was busy writing, though in declining health - over twenty books were published in his last decade. His theological writing was wide ranging, from a seven volume commentary on Hebrews, to books and articles on subjects relating to soteriology, and other vital doctrines. In *A Brief Declaration and Vindication of the Doctrine of the Trinity* first published in 1669 Owen writes for "edification and establishment of the plain Christian". He laid stress upon the practical import of doctrine in a Christian's life even when writing on subjects such as the Trinity.

Meditations and Discourses on the Glory of Christ was his final work. On the last day of his life William Payne, a minister from Saffron Walden, visited Owen and told him that the book was going to press. Owen's response was memorable: "*I am glad to hear it; but O brother Payne! The long wished for day is come at last, in which I shall see that glory in another manner than I have ever done, or was capable of doing in this world*". In the evening he departed to be with Christ.

His mortal body was buried on 4th September 1683 in Bunhill Fields, the Nonconformist burial ground then just outside the City of London, where John Bunyan would be buried almost exactly five years later.

JB

Footnotes

1. Laud was accused of treason and imprisoned in the Tower of London in 1641. A desperate need for finance had forced King Charles I to summon Parliament in November 1640. The majority in this 'Long Parliament' was determined to reverse Laud's policies and to limit the power of the Crown. Laud was impeached but in his trial no verdict could be reached. Parliament later passed a *Bill of Attainder* under which he was beheaded on 10th January 1645 at Tower Hill.

Information from *A Puritan's Mind* at www.apuritansmind.com and from *The Trinitarian Devotion of John Owen* by Sinclair B Ferguson, Reformation Trust

CHAPTER 14

The 18ᵗʰ Century

There can be no doubt that in every century of the Christian era God raised up faithful men who have been torchbearers of the Truth to their own generation. God never leaves Himself without a witness! The names of many are not known to us, particularly from the dark ages in the first millennium of the Christian era, but their record is on high.

The Reformation and immediate Post Reformation periods covered in previous chapters were in the main "troublous times" and a number of these noble witnesses to the Truth suffered martyrdom. Moving forward chronologically into the 18ᵗʰ century we shall see the new and different challenges to torchbearing. The fires of persecution were no longer burning in this country. Threats of imprisonment, torture or martyrdom had receded, but faithful men would now need to lift the torch of truth high in the face of rationalism and indifference.

Political Events

In the transition to this new era, recognisably modern in various aspects, two political events of great significance had taken place. The first occurred in 1689, the year following the death of John Bunyan, and became known as **The Glorious Revolution**. After the death of Cromwell, the monarchy had been restored and Charles II was crowned king in 1660. Charles died in 1685, and was succeeded by his brother James Duke of York who reigned as James II. James had previously made public his conversion to Catholicism and his accession as a Catholic monarch caused grave concern and anxiety. It soon became clear that James was bent upon a policy of authoritarian monarchy and the restoration in Britain of the Roman Catholic religion. The birth of a son baptised with Roman rites as James Francis Edward Stuart (later known as the Old Pretender) on 10th June 1688 hastened events which ultimately led to the flight of James, his wife Mary of Modena and their infant son to France, and then the coronation of William III and Mary II (elder daughter of James II by his first wife Anne Hyde) as joint monarchs on 11th April 1689. In the same year the Declaration of Rights limited the authority of the Crown, and an Act of Toleration secured religious freedom within certain bounds. It may be said that in the providence of God the groundwork was thus laid upon which rests our liberty to preach the Gospel and to live and meet as Christians. That such liberty has been enjoyed in this country for over three hundred years is no guarantee that it will continue, at least in the long accustomed fashion. We should therefore not only cherish our liberties in the Gospel, and pray for their continuance, but ensure that we make good use of them.

The second important event was **The Act of Union** in 1707 in terms of which the Scottish Parliament ceased to exist. This Act enabled Scottish members to sit in the House of Commons and in the House of Lords at Westminster. It has been said that the union was a political necessity for England and an economic one for Scotland. To appreciate the former point a brief resume of happenings since the accession of William and Mary is helpful. In 1701 the English parliament had passed the Act of Settlement, the purpose of which was to secure a Protestant Succession of the Crown. Mary had died in 1694 and her husband William in 1702. The crown then passed to Queen Anne, younger daughter of James II, who became the last monarch of the House of Stuart. It was seen to be extremely unlikely that she would have a surviving heir and in that event the nearest Protestant successor would be Sophia, Electress of Hanover, a first cousin to James II.

Sophia died in the same year as Anne, and her son succeeded to the throne as George I. The Whig party in England was determined that a Catholic Stuart would not succeed to the throne, however it was by no means certain that an independent Scots parliament would acquiesce in the choice of a Hanoverian successor to Queen Anne. It was feared that the loyalty of many Scots to the House of Stuart would lead to the Catholic son of James II becoming King James VIII of Scotland. This was the English driving force for the Union of Parliaments just over a century after the Union of the Crowns in 1603. It brought into being a United Kingdom with a constitutional monarchy for which a Protestant Succession was secured. The Hanoverian kings were not universally popular but successive Jacobite rebellions failed to undo the result of the Union.

Religious Life

The political and religious temper of 18th century Britain was set by the events described above. During the Protectorate, Oliver Cromwell had expressed his desire for "a free and uninterrupted Passage of the Gospel running through the midst of us and Liberty for all to hold forth and profess with sobriety their Light and Knowledge therein, according as the Lord in His rich Grace and Wisdom hath dispensed to every man and with the same freedom to practice and exercise the Faith of the Gospel and lead quiet and peaceable lives in all Godliness and Honesty without any interruption from the Powers God hath set over this Commonwealth". The ideal of Cromwell's aspirations may not have been fully realised, however the political and religious strife of the 16th and 17th centuries had given place to more settled conditions. Dissenters, i.e., people who were not members of the established churches, still suffered discrimination in a number of respects. Nevertheless there was now a significant measure of liberty for worship and witness, excepting Roman Catholics. It was not until as late as the early 19th century that the Catholic Emancipation Act was passed by Parliament during the Tory government of the Duke of Wellington.

As the 18th century progressed, apathy and barrenness descended upon the spiritual and religious life of the nation. This was due, in part at least, to the influence and patronage of the nobility or landed gentry in clerical appointments in the established churches. This could result in men of little ability or interest, or even unconverted men, filling pulpits. An example of the patronage of the local squire was caricaturised by the essayist Joseph Addison (1672 -1719) in *Sir Roger de Coverley at Church*.[1] In tandem with the spiritual barrenness and poverty of much of the Christian ministry there rose an unprecedented secular spirit in the public life of the nation. Rationalism and atheism began to spread their baneful influence. It was the so called "Age of Reason" when the writings of philosophers and free thinkers like David Hume and Jean-Jacques Rousseau gained currency in the minds of many.

A Dawning Light

In the milieu of spiritual slumber and rationalism God was working in ways that would transform Britain and achieve long lasting results. A bright light already shone in the life of Isaac Watts who became known as *"the father of English hymnody"*. His hymns gave utterance to spiritual emotions and aspirations in a way previously unknown in Britain. By his death in 1748 he had penned over six hundred hymns many of which remain well known to the present. Many great hymn writers followed in his train so that by the end of the century Christian praise and worship had been greatly enriched.

Furthermore a fresh blaze of Gospel truth was experienced through the labours of two men, John Wesley born in 1703, and George Whitefield born in 1714. By their prodigious labours the Gospel was made known and through the power of the Spirit of God multitudes were saved both in Britain and in British North America. It is interesting to reflect that God opened a wide channel of praise and worship for His people through a new richness of hymnology, and also met the spiritual plight of a multitude of souls in darkness by raising up the powerful Gospel testimony of Wesley and Whitefield. The spiritual impetus of these times had a far reaching influence upon the lives of future generations. The cumulative effect of successive times of revival in Britain has placed enormous responsibility upon this nation adding to the pathos of its moral and spiritual collapse in the second half of the 20th century.

JB

Footnote

1. *Selected English Essays* – chosen and selected by W. Peacock

CHAPTER 15

John Wesley (1703-1791)

In the year following the accession of Queen Anne a son was born to the Revd Samuel Wesley, rector of Epworth, a market town in the northern part of Lincolnshire, and his wife Susanna. He was named John, fifteenth in a large family of nineteen children of whom only seven survived. His origins were humble and relatively obscure yet God was to raise him up and use him in a mighty way as He had done with Gideon of old.

Susanna was a pious and intelligent woman who strictly disciplined her children and furnished them with the basis of a good education. In 1714, John at the age of eleven was sent to Charterhouse School in London, from which he went up to Christ Church Oxford to study with a view to ordination in the Church of England. He later became a fellow of Lincoln College Oxford. Although not yet saved by the grace of God, John and his younger brother Charles applied themselves seriously to devout living in the university. Such behaviour was much contrary to the common trend, and the strictness and regularity of their habits soon brought ridicule and scorn. They and their associates became known as "the Holy Club" or "Methodists".[1]

Georgia and the Moravians

In 1735 John and Charles Wesley accepted an invitation to sail over the Atlantic to the colony of Georgia established in 1732 by charter from King George II (after whom it was named). One object in founding the colony was to provide a haven for persecuted continental Protestants which explains the presence of Moravian settlers on board ship on the outward voyage.

Wesley was deeply impressed by the spiritual demeanour and calm of these Moravians particularly in the middle of a tempest encountered on the voyage. He recognised they possessed an inner strength which he lacked. On arrival at Savannah, capital of the new colony on 8th February 1736, Wesley took up his post as parish minister and missionary in the region. The mission was unsuccessful and John, beset with problems and disappointments, returned to England with Charles in February 1738.

In London he continued his association with the Moravians and it was at a Moravian meeting in Aldersgate Street on 24th May 1738 that John Wesley at last had a true conversion experience.[2] He heard a reading of Martin Luther's preface to the Epistle to the Romans and in his own oft quoted words, "I felt my heart strangely warmed ... an assurance was given me that He had taken away my sins even mine". It was the key to the rest of his life. A few weeks later he preached a sermon on the doctrine of personal salvation by faith, which was followed by another, on God's grace "free in all, and free for all". In October he wrote to Charles, "With regard to my own character and my doctrine likewise, I shall answer you very plainly. By a Christian I mean one who so believes in Christ as that sin has no more dominion over him; and in this obvious sense I was not a Christian till May, the 24th last. For till then sin had dominion over me, although I fought with it continually, but surely then, from that time to this it hath not, such is the free grace of God in Christ".

Around this time George Whitefield, finding church buildings closed to him, had begun preaching in fields to large crowds and he encouraged Wesley to do likewise. Initially Wesley was reluctant, but soon recognised that open air services were successful in reaching people who even then would not enter any of the churches. On 2nd April 1739 he went forth as an open air preacher and commenced a ministry of 52 years in which he declared "I look upon all the world as my parish". He took the opportunity to preach wherever congregations gathered, and more than once used his father's tombstone at Epworth as a pulpit. Wesley possessed many gifts, including that of organisation and leadership, but his greatest work was as an evangelist. His preaching, and that of Whitefield, led to a great evangelical revival in Britain and the American colonies.

His Preaching

Wesley frequently declared that he preached the fundamental principles of Christianity, and when pressed to define these he answered "the doctrine of justification by faith and that of the new birth". He also declared the doctrine of the assurance of salvation, teaching that with the forgiveness of sins there should also be experienced the inward assurance of the fact. He held high the torch of Gospel truth and testimony when sorely needed in that age of vice and debauchery so shockingly depicted in the famous engravings of William Hogarth. Open air meetings at that time were often interrupted by mobs that sometimes violently disturbed the preaching but Wesley was fearless and indefatigable in his labours. He travelled miles on horseback and preached twice and sometimes three or four times every day at a time when even with some improvement to the major turnpike roads, journeys remained arduous and dangerous.

Wesley preached the Gospel in *"plain words to plain folks"*, and had a deep compassion for poor working people, unchurched and uneducated. Seeing the enormous scale of the task throughout the country, he quickly recognised the need to encourage others to preach the Gospel. His appointments of men as lay preachers, not ordained or licensed by the Anglican Church, alarmed the Establishment and some of the clergy did not hesitate to make scurrilous and unfounded accusations against Wesley and his associates. Although the activities of these laymen were strictly controlled and organised into local circuits, it is fair to recognise a trend away from the restrictiveness and formality of clericalism towards a freer ministry by gifted persons of suitable moral and spiritual calibre.

Divergence did emerge between Wesley who held Arminian views, prevalent at that time in the Church of England, and

Whitefield who was a staunch Calvinist. None the less a warm and mutual regard prevailed between those two great men. Wesley preached Whitefield's funeral sermon in 1770. In the course of the 1770s, theological dispute broke out anew. Many pamphlets were issued by persons ranged on both sides of the controversy. Prominent on the Calvinist side were Augustus Toplady, Rowland Hill and Lady Huntingdon. Wesley's Arminian position was not extreme, and his concern seems to have been to defend the biblical doctrine of an unlimited atonement. He stated "All people can be saved. All people can know that they are saved. All people can be saved to the uttermost". From the perspective of our much later times we can salute the work and witness of all of those great figures and appreciate the way in which they were used by God in the fresh blaze of evangelism in the 18th century.

As the Abolitionist movement developed in Britain, Wesley spoke out and wrote against the slave trade. He was not afraid to declaim slavery publicly in the major slave port of Bristol. In one of his pamphlets on the subject he wrote "Liberty is the right of every human creature, as soon as he breathes the vital air; and no human law can deprive him of that right which he derives from the law of nature".

Into Old Age

Wesley enjoyed robust health through a long life being able to engage in a preaching tour from Aberdeen to Bristol in May to July 1790 when 87 years old. Throughout his busy life of travelling and preaching he kept a journal of almost daily entries for close to sixty years. He was a man of outstanding presence though small of stature, being less than 5 ft 5 ins tall. A contemporary described him thus: "He possessed a clear smooth forehead, an aquiline nose, eyes the brightest and most piercing imaginable, and a fresh complexion expressive of perfect health. His whole aspect crowned with a head as white as snow and clothed with an air of neatness and cleanliness, gave an idea of something primitive and apostolic".

He died in London on 2nd March 1791 and among his final words to those at his bedside were, *"The best of all, God is with us"*.

John Wesley's life spanned almost the whole of the 18th century and there is no doubt that he ranks as one of the great men of his era. His impact upon the public life of the nation was of course of a moral and spiritual character. Randall Davidson, Archbishop of Canterbury opined, "He was one of the greatest Englishmen who ever lived. It is not too much to say that Wesley changed the outlook, even the character of the English nation." (*The Times*, 2nd Nov 1928)

JB

Footnotes

1. Helpful information obtained from *Great Churchmen (No7)* by W Leathem, issued by the Church Society Trust.

2. A large plaque with more details marks the place in London today.

CHAPTER 16

Charles Wesley (1707 – 1788)

At rare intervals in our national life, Divine Providence has singularly gifted natural brothers to function with great distinction in their generation. The Wesleys in England in the 18th century and the Bonars in Scotland in the 19th are significant examples, and an interesting similarity may be noted. In each case while the brothers were gifted preachers, one was endowed pre-eminently with the spirit of poetry. Thus Charles Wesley and Horatius Bonar are remembered today principally as hymn writers. Many of their finest compositions continue in general use, a legacy of abiding spiritual value to Christians giving us a means of expressing emotions, desires, praise and worship. It is beyond dispute that Charles Wesley has been one of the greatest of hymn writers in the English language. His output was prodigious: 4,480 hymns were published in his lifetime, a very large number being of high merit.

Early Life and Conversion

Like his older brother John (see previous chapter), Charles was born in the rectory at Epworth, Lincolnshire, the eighteenth child in the family. He left home when eight years old to attend Westminster School, the *alma mater* of many famous men, where he was a bright and lively scholar gaining appointment as captain of the school. His education continued as a typically carefree student at Oxford. In his third year however he adopted a serious mode of life and study, and through his influence upon two other students, he formed an association which soon became ridiculed and called by others "the Holy Club".

The strict religious practices of Charles Wesley and his friends, commendable in many respects, were nevertheless in reality an effort to establish their own righteousness, and consequently brought neither joy nor peace to their souls. In due course Charles graduated and after a period employed as a tutor took "holy orders" preparatory to sailing with his brother to Georgia. There he met German Moravian Christians, and saw in these believers a calm assurance of faith he did not possess. The mission in Georgia was not a success and disappointed he returned to England, where in London came under the influence of the Moravian, Count Zinzendorf.

It was on Whitsunday 1738 that Charles at last was born again, just a few days prior to John's conversion. He had been studying the Epistle to the Galatians with Luther's commentary on it, and on the text at chapter 2 verse 20 he dwelt long "on this little word **me**". This led him to recognise the absolute necessity of personal faith in Christ, and believing he found rest to his soul.

His conversion became the stimulus for an outpouring of evangelical hymns and spiritual songs, the product of a heart on fire for God, a warm and emotional nature, and a genius for writing verse. Many of the early hymns were sung at the open air meetings when Whitefield and the Wesleys preached to large crowds:

> *All ye that pass by,*
> *To Jesus draw nigh;*
> *To you is it nothing that Jesus should die?*
> *Your ransom and peace,*
> *Your surety He is.*
> *Come see if there ever was sorrow like His.*

Revival Singing and Preaching

Such were the songs of the revival, expressing the sheer joy and vibrancy of salvation. The hearty singing of large congregations out of doors was unprecedented in that age, and must have been a soul stirring experience for all present. Charles Wesley's gifts found a ready outlet as he enthusiastically preached with power and to great effect in churches, where these were opened to him, and out of doors.

He also had a deep interest in prison work. The regime then existing in prisons was harsh to an extreme, with overcrowding and resulting unsanitary conditions adding to prisoners' misery. Undeterred Wesley went into prisons such as Newgate Gaol in London where on one occasion, laying aside previous prejudice against deathbed conversions, he preached to ten men under sentences of death. The men were saved and a week or so later he accompanied them to Tyburn where with "calm triumph" they went to the gallows. On the way they sang hymns including one written by the Wesleys' father:

> *Behold the Saviour of mankind,*
> *Nailed to the shameful tree!*
> *How vast the love that Him inclined*
> *To bleed and die for thee!*

We can only imagine the impression that must have been made on the crowds that witnessed such a scene.

Married Life

In the course of his travels Wesley met and courted a young Welsh woman named Sarah, whose father Marmaduke Gwynne was a wealthy magistrate living near Brecon, South Wales. Mr Gwynne had been converted through the ministry of the well known Welsh evangelist Howell Harris. Charles and Sarah, known as Sally, were married on 8th April 1749 and soon after set up home in Bristol. Sally was twenty-three years old, eighteen years younger than her husband, but well suited to support him in his spiritual endeavours, and they enjoyed a most happy marriage. For some time Wesley was accompanied on his itinerant preaching tours by his wife who rode behind him on a pillion, and whose fine voice led the singing.

In December 1753 Sally contracted the dreaded smallpox. Charles was preaching in London, and the Countess of Huntingdon, who at that time was living nearby, bravely visited

Sally twice daily even when her condition deteriorated and her life hung in the balance. This was only ten years after two of Lady Huntingdon's children had died of smallpox, but her care for Sally continued until Charles returned and Sally's mother was present. Sally did recover but sadly her son Jacky caught the infection and died only sixteen months old. Of their eight children only three survived infancy. Such events were all too common in those days!

Remarkable Hymns

Deep soul experience with God, in sorrow and in joy, in trials and in triumphs, lent richness to hymns covering a wide range of spiritual subjects.

The yearning of a storm tossed soul for refuge and comfort echoes in the lovely words:

> *Jesus, Lover of my soul,*
> *Let me to Thy bosom fly,*
> *While the nearer waters roll,*
> *While the tempest still is high;*
> *Hide me, O my Saviour, hide,*
> *Till the storm of life is past;*
> *Safe into the haven guide,*
> *Oh receive my soul at last!*

The heart of every believer is surely lifted up in praise when singing:

> *Oh for a thousand tongues to sing*
> *My great Redeemer's praise;*
> *The glories of my God and King,*
> *The triumphs of His grace.*

In his famous carol *Hark! the herald angels sing,* Wesley takes us to the heart of the doctrine of the incarnation of our Lord Jesus Christ in the lines:

> *Late in time behold Him come,*
> *Offspring of a virgin's womb;*
> *Veiled in flesh the Godhead see;*
> *Hail th' Incarnate Deity.*

In 1771 Charles moved to London where he exercised a pastoral ministry among the Societies of Christians in the capital. He preached twice on most Sundays in the City Road Chapel, after it opened in November 1778. In later years his powers as a preacher waned, but not his ability to write verse. At the beginning of 1788 his strength began to fail and he died on 29th March of that year. He was buried in the churchyard of St Marleybone.

Charles Wesley's hymns were his greatest contribution to the mighty work of God of his own day, and Christians the world over still rejoice in those hymns included in the major collections presently in use. Fourteen appear in *The Believer's Hymn Book* and twelve are found in *Hymns of Light and Love*. Thus we share in Wesley's spiritual legacy!

But when we sing *And can it be that I should gain an interest in the Saviour's blood?,* or *Love divine, all loves excelling*, or any of his other hymns, we are not of Wesley! Rather Wesley is ours, just in the sense that Paul meant when, in rebuking the sectarian spirit within the assembly of God at Corinth he wrote,

> Therefore let no man glory in men. For all things are yours:
>
> Whether Paul, or Apollos, or Cephas, or the world, or life, or death, or things present, or things to come; all are yours;
>
> And ye are Christ's and Christ is God's.

(1 Cor 3.21-23)

JB

CHAPTER 17

George Whitefield (1714-1770)

On 9th May 1738 a vessel arrived in the Savannah river in the new colony of Georgia. It had been a lengthy voyage and no doubt all on board looked forward to setting foot on shore. Among the passengers was a young man of 23 years arriving in America for the first time. George Whitefield had already made his mark as a preacher and many had been astonished that he should leave England to sail to distant and primitive Georgia, but the Wesleys had encouraged him to come to help the Christian mission there and he had felt called to go. It was to be the first of seven visits to British North America, no mean feat almost a century before the advent of a regular steamship service on the North Atlantic or the building of the speedy clipper ships that rivalled the earlier steamers. The merchant vessels of Whitefield's day were in the main bluff bowed, deep drafted, and unable to sail close to the wind resulting in long passages especially west bound. His sea voyages and other travels evidenced a passion to preach the gospel, and led to George Whitefield becoming the first transatlantic evangelist, a torchbearer in the Old Country and in New England too.

Early Life

The early life of Whitefield gave no hint of his illustrious future. He was born on 16th December 1714 in the Bell Inn, Gloucester where his father was innkeeper. The year had seen the death of Queen Anne, the last Stuart monarch, and the accession of the Hanoverian King George I. But close to its end, the birth of George Whitefield would prove to be an event of great significance in the spiritual realm. We may discern that God's ways are behind the scenes, but He moves all the scenes which He is behind, and ponder the import of that in our nation's history.

When he was 12 years old George was sent to St Mary de Crypt Grammar School in Gloucester, where he gained a reputation for oratory and acting, and for truancy! Later he persuaded his mother that he should leave school, thinking his education would be of little use to him, and for some time he worked in the inn. Happily he listened to good advice, reversed his earlier decision and returned to the Grammar School to prepare to go up to Pembroke College Oxford. At university he met Charles Wesley, became acquainted with the "Holy Club", and was drawn away from former sinful associates. It was a turning point in his life leading to his conversion in 1735 when he put his whole trust in the righteousness of the Lord Jesus Christ rather than upon the practices of the Holy Club. In after years he said, "I know the place. Whenever I go to Oxford I cannot help running to the spot where Jesus Christ first revealed himself to me, and gave me the new birth."

Following ordination in June 1736 he preached for the first time in the ancient church of St Mary de Crypt in Gloucester where he had grown up. Whitefield was diligent in study, earnest in prayer and soon he was called to London to act as a supply minister and began preaching with power to large congregations.

Powerful Preaching

His first visit to Georgia followed this period, but by December 1738 Whitefield was back in London. He was dismayed to find many churches and pulpits closed to him as his clear preaching of the doctrines of justification by grace through faith alone, and the necessity of the work of the Holy Spirit in regeneration, had offended many. This led directly to open air preaching, and on 17th February 1739 at Kingswood Hill, a coal mining district near to Bristol he preached to around 200 rough and ready miners. Soon a large number were professing salvation and demonstrating the reality of their profession by changed lives.

Whitefield declared "Having no righteousness of their own to renounce they were glad to hear of a Jesus who was friend to publicans and came not to call the righteous but sinners to repentance".

Soon he was preaching to thousands in fair weather and foul. It is recorded that crowds often stood in the rain listening, and that the melody of their singing could be heard two miles away. Some opposed and scorned, and Whitefield records "I was honoured with having stones, dirt, rotten eggs and pieces of dead cats thrown at me". More polite opposition came from the Bishop of London, who denounced Whitefield and his preaching, but the Great Awakening had begun, and the light of the Gospel blazed forth upon a scene of appalling moral and spiritual darkness.

Considering the state of society in the early eighteenth century one can see parallels with the present. The concept of truth received by revelation was utterly rejected by many who asserted that truth was only to be found through reason. The Church of England was afflicted with various heterodoxies, and the consequence of it all was rank unbelief, which inevitably led to immorality, corruption, and crime. Many were sucked into a vortex of materialism, avarice and corruption, or of debauchery, drunkenness and vice in which gratification of the basest desires stripped men and women of every vestige of decency, and ruined both mind and body. The preaching of Whitefield and others led to deliverance for thousands who believed the gospel, repented, and trusted the Lord Jesus Christ. Staid and unregenerate clergy criticised what they regarded as the excesses of Revivalism, unable to recognise real work being wrought through the power of the Spirit of God.

Revivals

Revival was soon to be seen in an even more remarkable way in New England. In August 1739 Whitefield departed on his second voyage to America, arriving this time in Philadelphia where he preached to large numbers from the balcony of the Court House. After visiting New York he journeyed south through Maryland and

Carolina to Georgia. He founded an orphanage in Savannah named Bethesda having been deeply concerned for homeless children. In September 1740 he sailed north to New England. The well known Jonathan Edwards had been preaching in Rhode Island to great effect, but the arrival of Whitefield brought an unprecedented wave of blessing to the colony. He preached on Boston Common to the largest crowds that had yet assembled there. At Old North Church thousands were turned away so he took the message out of doors. It was the same at Salem and at Northampton, Massachusetts, where he preached in Edward's church. In all these places revival continued for months after Whitefield returned to England.

Soon after his return he visited Scotland for the first time. In Glasgow many were brought under deep conviction as he preached. At Cambuslang he addressed his largest ever audience, estimated as 100,000. We may wonder whether so many could hear, but Whitefield possessed a powerful voice and spoke with clarity and conviction. He preached in Wales where he met Elizabeth James, an older widow, whom he married in November 1741. Their only son John was born in 1743 but died only four months old. In 1756 he visited Ireland where he suffered violent opposition. One Sunday afternoon while preaching near Dublin, stones and dirt were thrown at him. A mob gathered and some fled the scene, leaving him to walk nearly half a mile alone while rioters threw showers of stones upon him until he was covered in blood. He was able to stagger to a minister's door where he found shelter. He often said, *"We are immortal till our work is done."*

Last Visit to Georgia

And so Whitefield laboured with energy and enthusiasm, God using him in a mighty way for His glory and the blessing of countless souls throughout Great Britain and North America.

Late in 1769 he sailed for Georgia to arrange for the orphanage in Savannah to be converted to Bethesda College. In the spring of 1770 he travelled on to New England. At every place he was warmly received, crowds flocking to hear him preach. In Boston he was ill for a time but became able to continue further, and at length arrived in Newburyport, Massachusetts on 29th September where he had supper with Rev. Jonathan Parsons. He went to bed unwell and by 2am he was struggling to breathe. He died early on Sunday 30th September, and was buried beneath the pulpit of the Old South Presbyterian Church of Newburyport.

Whitefield was certainly a great preacher, but equally his Christ-like spirit caused him to be greatly esteemed by his contemporaries. John Wesley exclaimed "Oh, what has the church suffered in the setting of that bright star which shone so gloriously in our hemisphere. We have none left to succeed him; none of his gifts; none anything like him in usefulness".

JB

CHAPTER 18

Selina Countess of Huntingdon (1707 – 1791)

"For ye see your calling, brethren, how that not many wise men after the flesh, not many mighty, not many noble are called" (1 Cor 1.26). The Countess quoting the verse is reputed to have exclaimed *"I'm glad it says not many, rather than not any"*. Many others, similarly glad, had cause to rejoice that God had called a peeress of the realm to play a notable role in the great Evangelical Awakening of the 18th century. William Grimshaw a noted Yorkshire preacher (see Chapter 19) wrote "He has raised you up for the accomplishment of a mighty work in the land. I may not live to witness it, but I shall assuredly see some of the triumphs of the cross, the blood bought slaves, the ransomed captives, rescued from the tyranny and slavery of the great enemy of souls in the chapels of your Ladyship, all arrayed in robes of dazzling white, and washed from every defilement in the fountain opened for sin and unclean-ness, praising and blessing Him who hath made them kings and priests unto God and the Lamb for ever". How did all this come about?

Aristocratic Background

Selina Shirley was born at Astwell Manor House, a family property near Brackley in Northamptonshire in 1707. The Shirley family was of ancient lineage stretching back to Saxon times, with possessions in various parts of England and Ireland. Selina's paternal grandmother Elizabeth Washington was also of an old and respected family some of whom had emigrated in

1657. George Washington, first President of the United States descended from the American branch of that family. Disputes, particularly between Selina's grandfather and the children of his first marriage, disturbed family life. When Selina was only six years old her parents separated and her mother took her youngest daughter and left Britain to spend the rest of her life abroad. Selina became strongly attached to her father, but in contrast, correspondence with her mother was formal. In later life she rarely spoke of her childhood but some anecdotes reveal a serious minded child with a sense of eternity. In her teens, as thoughts turned toward marriage, she prayed that she might marry into a serious family, and God answered her prayer.

Donington Hall not far distant from Selina's home, was the seat of Theophilus Hastings Ninth Earl of Huntingdon. The two families were acquainted and following the formalities of the time Selina and Theophilus married on 3rd June 1728. It proved to be a happy and loving marriage. The young couple enjoyed the pursuits of the nobility common in those days, such as attending court in London, moving between their country homes and estates and taking the waters at Bath. Blessed with a growing family, their lives were leisured and privileged. However the Countess was feeling an increasing sense of the emptiness of life and finding no lasting satisfaction in its pleasures. Unknown to her, events were then occurring that would lead to her life being transformed.

Conversion

A young man Benjamin Ingham, converted while in Georgia, had returned to England and was preaching the Gospel in his home town Ossett in Yorkshire. This resulted in many people being stirred up to seek salvation by faith alone. Earl Huntingdon's sisters lived in the area at Ledston Hall and in due course Ingham received an invitation to preach in the private chapel there. The Hastings sisters were brought under conviction and soon Lady Margaret was saved, followed by her sisters Anne and Frances. When in June 1739 the Earl and Countess visited Ledston Hall, Lady Margaret declared "Since I have known and believed in the Lord Jesus Christ for salvation, I have been as happy as an angel". Selina, becoming aware of her inadequacies to merit salvation, was deeply moved and recognised that her sister-in-law had joy and peace to which she was a stranger. After struggle and anxiety, remembering Lady Margaret's words, Selina cast herself wholly upon Christ for life and salvation on 26th July 1739.

She commenced the serious study of Scripture and the effect soon became manifest in her conduct. News spread rapidly, amid ridicule and scorn that she had been converted by "The Methodists" as the preachers had become known. Selina was to suffer much obloquy and reproach from those who judged that she had betrayed her class and departed from the traditions of the Church. Theophilus seems not to have attained the same degree of understanding of the Gospel as his wife, but there is no evidence that he ever discouraged her spiritual aims or her support of Christian work. He died on 13th October 1746, only 50 years of age. Four months later Selina wrote to Philip Doddridge the well known Dissenting minister and hymn writer "I dread slack hands in the vineyard; we must all up and be doing". She later wrote "O! How I do lament the weakness of my knees and coolness of my heart! I want [my heart] on fire always, not for self delight, but to spread the gospel from pole to pole". She strove to accomplish that goal by three principal means.

Christian Service

The Countess made it possible for members of the aristocracy to hear the Gospel preached with clarity and power. As a peeress she had a legal right to appoint two private chaplains to minister to the spiritual needs of her household. She invited George Whitefield to become her chaplain and when he accepted she began to invite members of the nobility, politicians and even Frederick, Prince of Wales to her Chelsea home in London to hear him preach. Other well known preachers including John Wesley and William Romaine addressed these gatherings which continued for many years. Refreshment on these occasions was limited to drinks of tea and lemonade but this did not deter many prominent people attending. In the scale of the revival of the mid eighteenth century the number saved was comparatively small, but the impact was significant in combating atheism, rationalism, and indifference among the governing class. A significant case of conversion was the Earl of Dartmouth, later to become Colonial Secretary and fill other important offices. In 1755 he heard George Whitefield preaching and was converted. He used his substantial means in support of evangelical testimony and became an advocate for the Gospel among the nobility and the court. William Cowper saluted Lord Dartmouth in the lines,

We boast some rich ones whom the gospel sways,
And one who wears a coronet and prays.

Another means by which the gospel progressed was by building chapels. The first to be built solely at the initiative of the Countess was in Brighton. It was intended that it should supplement and not replace the parish church, by providing extra preaching meetings at times other than the regular services. Over the years Lady Huntingdon devoted large sums of money to building or purchasing chapels in many places. Her lease in 1779 of Spa Fields Chapel in the Clerkenwell district in the northern outskirts of London accommodating congregations of 3,000 persons became a catalyst for change. The opposition of a local curate led to a case being brought before an Ecclesiastical Court where a verdict was reached prejudicial to the Countess's interest in that chapel and setting a precedent that put at risk the work elsewhere. After hesitation and with great regret the Countess decided to protect all her chapels under the 1689 Toleration Act, thereby making them Dissenting Meeting Houses. This decision led to the formation of the Huntingdon Connexion in the middle ground between the Established Church and Dissent. Many Anglican ministers who previously had been happy to preach in the chapels now felt unable to do so and severed their links with Lady Huntingdon. Naturally these events were disappointments to her but she remained undaunted by them.

Trevecca College

A related concern was the provision of men capable of preaching and ministering in the chapels. Lady Huntingdon had financially supported the studies of many promising young men, but at the age of over sixty she embarked upon one of her most enterprising projects, the founding of a college at Trevecca in Wales in 1768. Difficulties were encountered, but with determination and commitment these were overcome. It has been reckoned that about 230 studied there in the course of Selina's life. Periods of study were interposed with times when students preached as itinerants or filled vacancies in various chapels.

Soon after the founding of Trevecca College the Countess made a direct approach to King George III concerning the frivolities and entertainments being provided by Frederick Cornwallis, the incumbent Archbishop of Canterbury, and his wife. Cornwallis was an aristocrat who had enjoyed a smooth and rapid preferment in the Church. She did not shirk from telling the king that such frivolities were unacceptable. The King and Queen Charlotte had been anxious to meet the Countess and were impressed by her. They asked many questions about her work and the College. The king later remarked to Lord Dartmouth "I wish there was a Lady Huntingdon in every diocese in my kingdom", and he continued, "There is something so noble, so commanding and withal so engaging about her, that I am quite captivated with her Ladyship. She appears to possess talents of a very superior order – is clever, well informed and has all the ease and politeness belonging to her rank".

With unflagging zeal over many years Lady Huntingdon served the Lord Jesus Christ and into old age retained a vision for evangelism at home and abroad. As the century entered its last decade many friends and companions had already passed away. John Wesley finished his course in March 1791 by which time the Countess was close to her own rest. On 17th June 1791, the last day of her life, she said to her doctor, "My work is done. I have nothing to do but to go to my heavenly Father." As she wished she was buried in simplicity in an unmarked grave beside her husband in the family vault in Ashby-de-la-Zouch.

JB

Footnote

Selina Countess of Huntingdon by Faith Cook, Banner of Truth, provided much of the information for this chapter.

CHAPTER 19

William Grimshaw (1708 – 1763)

The village of Haworth situated in the bleak Pennine moorland of the West Riding of Yorkshire is internationally famous as having been the home of the Bronte sisters when their father Patrick Bronte was curate there. Emily, Charlotte and Anne were the authors respectively of *Jane Eyre*, *Wuthering Heights* and *The Tenant of Wildfell Hall*. Two generations earlier a man of God, William Grimshaw, ministered at Haworth church. His name is not as well known the Brontes, nor as Whitefield's, or the Wesleys who travelled more widely, but he was greatly used of God, particularly in Yorkshire during the "Great Awakening".

Early Life and Ordination

Grimshaw was born in Brindle, a hamlet to the south west of Blackburn in Lancashire. In early life he had some spiritual concerns, but these waned as he grew up. After education at a public school in Blackburn he went up to Christ's College, Cambridge, where for two years he was a sober and diligent student before falling into bad company and habits. After graduating he was ordained curate for a short time at Rochdale and then in 1732 at Todmorden about eight miles west of Halifax. His ungodly lifestyle was at that time no bar to ordination by the Church of England. Like not a few of its clergy he had little sense of vocation and enjoyed the pursuits of the local gentry such as hunting, shooting and card playing. Occasionally Grimshaw suffered pangs of conscience but these were smothered until an extraordinary experience befell him.

James Scholfield was a local hill farmer whose wife Susan

bore a son after ten years of marriage. Their delight gave way to despair when the child became sick, and fearful for his life they arranged for his baptism when he was just five weeks old. The parents were distraught when their son died on the day of his baptism. Being devout and regular in their attendance at church it was natural for them to look to the Revd Grimshaw for solace and spiritual comfort. They found neither, for the unregenerate Grimshaw was incapable of helping. His shallow advice was visit friends, eat, drink and make merry. Grimshaw began to feel remorse and shame for his own inadequacies. He recognised his utter failure to help his parishioners and the incident marked a turning point in his life. The story had a happy ending as the Scholfields lived to be over eighty and had two more daughters and two healthy sons. Most importantly they both became earnest Christians and Grimshaw later wrote to them, "What a blind leader of the blind I was when I came to take off thy burden, by exhorting thee to live in pleasure and to follow the vain amusements of the world! But God has in His mercy pardoned and blessed us all three. Blessed be His great name!"

Grimshaw forsook his easy going lifestyle and began to seriously devote himself to his religious duties. His sermons warned his congregations of their spiritual danger, and urged upon them upright living to obtain favour with God. He began to record his conduct in order to monitor it more strictly. This continued for seven years but brought no rest to his troubled conscience.

During this period Grimshaw married a young widow, Sarah Sutcliffe in 1735. A son was born followed by a daughter, and domestic happiness distracted him for a time, but soon heart searchings reasserted themselves. He was nigh overwhelmed by sorrow when Sarah died in 1739. The children were cared for by his wife's relatives and Grimshaw now alone in his parsonage, desolate and broken in spirit, despaired of ever finding an end to his spiritual conflict. An itinerant minister frequently passed through the area, and rebuked Grimshaw for his legalistic views of salvation telling him often, "Mr Grimshaw you are building on the sand." The words burned in his mind.

Conversion and Revival Preaching

One day in 1741 he saw in a friend's home a book titled *The Doctrine of Justification by Faith* written by the Puritan John Owen. Reading this book Grimshaw found the answer to his problem. As he described later "I was now willing to renounce myself, every degree of fancied merit and ability, and to embrace Christ only for my all in all. O what light and comfort did I now enjoy in my soul, and what a taste of the pardoning love of God". New life infused his ministry as extempore prayer mingled with the set prayers of the liturgy, and as he preached Christ as the Saviour of sinners. Like many another, Grimshaw was assailed by doubts and fears but was greatly helped by a Scotsman William Darney known as "Scotch Will". Darney, a shoemaker and peddler, travelled around the villages preaching the gospel. Grimshaw initially had reservations about Darney's preaching, possibly because he was not ordained, however he warmed to Darney and in humility was willing to learn from him. He found that Darney enjoyed the assurance that he was "sealed unto the day of redemption", a truth at the time little known, and Grimshaw learned not to lean upon his own feelings but on the unchanging Word of God.

His move to Haworth took place the spring of 1742. This small town and the surrounding area were to become the scene of a remarkable outpouring of revival showers upon dry ground. News of the earnest and powerful preaching of the new curate at Haworth spread abroad and before long the congregations were so large that hundreds had to stand in the churchyard. The spiritual conflicts of earlier times brought a depth and warmth to his ministry. Though well educated he addressed his congregations in basic terms ensuring that his message was understood "If you perish, you will perish [and in broad Yorkshire dialect] wi' t' sound o' t' gospel i' yer lugs!" He preached with passion and solemnity, "God still waits to be gracious to you and takes pleasure in showing mercy. His patience bears, His justice forbears, His mercy entreats. Christ stands offering His blood and merits freely to you. The Holy Spirit is persuading you; ministers are calling and praying for you; your conscience is accusing you; yea and the devil is waiting for your death that he may have you into hell". Those who heard his pulpit prayers were gripped by their reality. "He was like a man at times with his feet on earth and his soul in heaven. He would take hold of the horns of the altar and he would not let go until God had given the blessing." Little wonder souls were being saved!

For a time Grimshaw was reluctant to cross parish boundaries, but as people from neighbouring parishes continued to come to Haworth, so the demand for him to preach elsewhere increased. Convinced of the need, he began an evangelical and pastoral ministry throughout Yorkshire and into neighbouring counties. William Crabtree who later became a Baptist pastor was converted when a young man through Grimshaw's preaching. He described how Grimshaw conducted his itinerant ministry. "He divided the country into districts, taking one regularly each week. His usual manner was, upon entering the house, after having with uplifted hands pronounced a blessing upon the people assembled, to fall down upon his knees and pray with great fervency, and then preach with a plainness and pungency peculiarly adapted to his hearers, for a convenient space of time". He was glad to eat any food offered to him by the poor and humble folk of the district, sometimes a potato sprinkled with salt! Grimshaw had the care of souls at heart, visiting the scattered societies of believers. Though his admonitions were stern, his pleadings were tender, and his devoted care endeared him to all believers. Thus he became greatly loved and respected.

Opposition and Suffering

He experienced opposition, sometimes instigated by clergy who were jealous of his popularity. This broke into open violence during a visit by John Wesley in 1748 when rioters disrupted the preaching and one man struck Wesley across the face while another hit him over the head with a stick. Grimshaw too was roughly handled but was able to shake off his assailants. George Whitefield and others much used by God in the Great Awakening loved to visit Haworth, and loved and respected

Grimshaw. William Romaine's testimony was fulsome. He wrote, "Mr Grimshaw was the most laborious and indefatigable minister of Christ that I ever knew, and I believe one of the most so that ever was in England since the first preaching of the Gospel". Grimshaw viewed his service in a modest light. In a letter to Romaine in 1762 he wrote, "When I come to die, I shall have my greatest grief and my greatest joy – my greatest grief that I have done so little for Jesus; and my greatest joy that Jesus has done so much for me. My last words shall be: 'Here goes an unprofitable servant'."

William Grimshaw bore much sorrow in family life. His second wife Elizabeth died only five years after their marriage and subsequently his daughter died, aged twelve. He had been a strong, robust man, broad-shouldered and well-built, but in his early fifties he suffered increasing ill-health. He preached from his own pulpit for the last time on 20th March 1763. On the following day he realised that he had contracted typhus in an epidemic of the fever which had broken out in Haworth. In his weakened state he was unable to resist the ravages of his illness and on 7th April went to be with the Lord.

As he wished he was buried in a poor man's clothes and in a poor man's coffin with the words of Phil 1.21 inscribed upon the lid. He had asked that the funeral address be based upon that text. It was a fitting epithet: *For to me to live is Christ, and to die is gain.*

And there was a happy postscript! Grimshaw's son John, a wastrel and a drunkard, had broken his father's heart, but now, broken by remorse and regret, the prodigal found mercy and forgiveness. He exclaimed before he died just three years later, "*What will my father say when he sees me in heaven!*"

JB

Footnotes

1. *William Grimshaw of Haworth* by Faith Cook, Banner of Truth, provided much of the information for this chapter.

2. *Curate of Haworth*, an unpublished biography by James Everett

CHAPTER 20

John Berridge (1716 – 1793)

Most parts of the United Kingdom were affected by the great Evangelical Awakening of the 18th century. The labours of preachers such as the Wesleys and George Whitefield brought the Gospel to ordinary folks far and wide. But other men too, like William Grimshaw who preached in Yorkshire, and John Berridge, known as "the pedlar of the Gospel" in East Anglia, with many others, made a notable contribution to the work of the Lord in their day.

Early Life and Influences

John Berridge was the son of a wealthy Nottinghamshire farmer. Much of his childhood was spent with an aunt who was entrusted with his care. There seems to have been little spiritual influence in his early life but one day he was invited to the home of a fellow pupil with whom he had become friendly. While there the boy read a portion of scripture, which John deeply disliked. However he did not wish to offend his friend and so remained silent. His unease continued when the Bible was read on subsequent visits, but though the seed would remain dormant for many years it ultimately sprang up and bore fruit. How good to reflect upon the spiritual inclinations of an unknown schoolboy these many years ago, which caused him to read from the Bible to a friend. Around the time he left school John began to be conscious of his sinfulness and an interest in spiritual things was deepened by conversations he had with a Christian tailor in a nearby town.

At the age of fourteen John returned to his father's home. He showed no talent for farming and eventually his father accepted his son's lack of interest and permitted him to enter Clare College, Cambridge to study theology. The reasons behind Berridge's choice of course are not known, but he enjoyed study and achieved academic success, reading in addition to theology, logic, mathematics, and metaphysics. He obtained an MA degree, and was made a Fellow of Clare College in 1742. He moved in a wide social circle and became influenced by ideas and philosophies which distracted him from reading or studying scripture. In spite of this he was ordained in 1745, though at that time he felt no desire to take up any ecclesiastical responsibility. In 1749 perhaps because of an uneasy conscience he accepted appointment as curate at Stapleford near Cambridge. At that time he thought that human merit and virtue were adequate to obtain salvation and his lively sermons exhorted his congregations to a life of good works.

Turning Point

This very formal and ineffective ministry continued when he became vicar of Everton, a small village to the east of Bedford in 1755, but later in that year Berridge reached the great turning point of his life. Daily Bible study and meditation brought him to understand that striving to merit salvation by good works was sheer vanity and pride. The conviction "cease from thine own works, only believe", was impressed upon his heart and he grasped the glorious and liberating truth of justification by faith. His life was transformed and a new vitality and authority infused his ministry. He began to make up for the years he had wasted, and burning all his old carefully constructed sermons, determined with himself not to know anything among his people save Jesus Christ and Him crucified. The radical change quickly became apparent to his parishioners, and soon there were frequent conversions among the increasing numbers who heard him preach.

By 1758 Berridge was riding on horseback throughout the whole of Bedfordshire and neighbouring counties, preaching up to twelve times in a week, in villages, farms and in the open air. He went wherever people could be found, whether in large numbers or in smaller groups. He possessed an unwavering confidence that "God has promised a reformation when His word is truly preached". Like many of his contemporaries he experienced opposition, and often had to endure rowdy interruptions and insults, but was not dismayed, for he knew that the preaching of the cross would cause offence. He believed that the doctrines of grace "batter all human pride, undermine all human merit, lay the human worm in the dust, and give the glory of salvation wholly unto God".

Preaching the Word

Berridge's preaching beyond his own parish boundaries irritated and alarmed other clergy, but when Matthias Mawson, Bishop of Ely threatened to dispossess him if he did not cease his itinerant preaching, Berridge boldly sent a robust reply: "Since the gospel preachers are thinly scattered and neighbouring pulpits are locked up against them, then it behoves them to take advantage of fields, or barns or houses to cast abroad the gospel seed. There is one cannon which says 'Go preach the gospel to every creature'." Notwithstanding such opposition, Berridge remained steadfastly loyal to the Church of England. When in 1782 the Countess of Huntingdon decided to register her chapels as Dissenting Meeting Houses, Berridge was one of a number who no longer felt free to preach for her. This may now seem strange to us, but Berridge with Augustus Toplady and many others whose ministry was greatly blessed of the Lord in the salvation of many souls, viewed Dissent with horror, though they acknowledged there were godly men among Dissenters. They were convinced that the historic doctrines of the Church expressed in the *Thirty Nine Articles* were thoroughly scriptural. None the less we salute their devotedness to the Lord. They served Him well in the light they had.

Berridge's preaching was plain and pithy. "I asked them, if they had ever broken the law of God once in thought, word or deed? If they had, they were under the curse, 'for it is written, cursed is every one that continueth not in all things that are written in the book of the law to do them'. If I keep all God's laws today this is no amends for breaking them yesterday. If I behave peaceably to my neighbour this day, it is no satisfaction for having broken his head yesterday". Later he advised younger men, "Look simply to Jesus for preaching food: what is wanted will be given, and what is given will be blessed. Your mouth will be a flowing stream or a fountain sealed according as your heart is".

He was a zealous preacher and evidently an instrument of grace and power in the Lord's hand. Other noted evangelists rejoiced in the gracious work, and Berridge became highly esteemed by them. John Wesley noted that people "came now twelve or fourteen miles to hear him, and very few came in vain". Later, in 1776 the well known Henry Venn accompanied Berridge in a preaching tour and stated that he had "the largest congregations that were ever known, and greatly was his word owned of the Lord". George Whitefield, quoting scripture, said "he was a burning and a shining light". Lady Huntingdon often asked him to preach in her chapels, though he was not always disposed to go. He was not a man to be awed, writing to the Countess, "My Lady, I cannot see my call to Brighthelmstone; (the old name for Brighton) and I ought to see it for myself, not another for me…I write plainly, not out of forwardness, I trust, but to save your ladyship the trouble of sending a second request, and myself the pain of returning a second denial".

Personal Life

His determination not to marry was cogently expressed with some humour. He wrote, "There is no trap so mischievous to the field preacher as wedlock; and it is laid for him at every hedge corner." Few of the other preachers of his era shared this view!

Berridge wrote a number of hymns, a collection of which was published as *Original Sion's Songs.* Many were based upon Psalms or portions of Scripture.

For more than thirty years Berridge laboured in the Gospel with great effect, but ultimately both his sight and hearing began to fail. He died at the age of seventy seven and was buried in the Everton Churchyard. Thousands of people attended his funeral service at which Charles Simeon preached from 2 Tim 4.7, "I have fought a good fight, I have finished my course, I have kept the faith". He composed his own epitaph, a testimony inscribed upon his tombstone as follows:

Here lie the remains of John Berridge
late vicar of Everton
and an itinerant servant of Jesus Christ.
Who loved his Master and his work
and after running on His 'Errands' many years
was called up to wait on Him above.

Reader art thou born again?
No salvation without new birth.
I was born in sin February 1716
Remained ignorant of my fallen state till 1730.
Lived proudly on faith and works for salvation till 1754
Admitted to Everton vicarage 1755
Fled to Jesus alone for refuge 1756
Fell asleep in Christ 22 January 1793

JB

Footnote

Some information in this chapter from *The Works of the Revd. John Berridge including a Memoir of His life* by Richard Whittingham, 1838.

CHAPTER 21

William Romaine (1714 – 1795)

The strength of character of this remarkable man was captured by J C Ryle in his Preface to *Christian Leaders of the 18th Century*. Using the simile of an army to illustrate the differing ministries of four spiritual heroes raised up by God in the evangelical revivals he wrote, "Whitefield and Wesley were spiritual cavalry, who scoured the country, and were found everywhere. William Grimshaw was an infantry soldier, who had his headquarters in Haworth and never went far from home. Romaine was a commander of heavy artillery, who held a citadel in the heart of the metropolis, and seldom stirred beyond his walls."

Family History

William Romaine was of Huguenot stock. His grandfather Robert Romaine arrived in England from France shortly before the revocation of the Edict of Nantes in October 1685 by Louis XIV. This Edict, issued in 1598 by Louis' grandfather Henry IV, had protected the rights of French Calvinist Protestants often called Huguenots. It has been estimated that when the Edict was revoked around 400,000 Huguenots left France to settle in England, Holland, Prussia, North America and South Africa. Robert Romaine settled with his family in the small north east seaport of Hartlepool where William Romaine Snr became a well respected corn merchant. He and his wife Isabella had nine children of whom William born in 1714 (the same year as Whitefield) was the second. The children were reared in a happy Christian home.

Education

William received his early education at Kepier Grammar School, Houghton le Spring, which had been founded in 1557 by the Rector Bernard Gilpin, known as the Apostle of the North. It was a place of sound learning, and from there William went up to Hart Hall, now Hertford College Oxford, which numbered William Tyndale and John Donne among its famous former students. Romaine made great literary progress and studied the Scriptures in their original languages in preparation for ministry in the Church. At university he consorted with like minded scholars who followed and developed the views of one John Hutchinson (1674 – 1737) a High Church Anglican, who, from a mystical interpretation of Hebrew roots, taught that the Old Testament Scriptures embraced a complete system of natural philosophy and religion.

Such views coloured the early years of Romaine's ministry near Epsom. He became a noted Hebrew scholar and published a new edition of the Hebrew Concordance and Dictionary of F. Marius de Calasio (d. 1620) a learned professor of Hebrew at Rome. The new edition took ten years to complete and was published in four volumes. Romaine's grasp of Old Testament doctrine is revealed by the following, written when he was only twenty-six years old: "The law of Moses pointed out by its types and emblems the person of Christ. Particularly it pointed him out by sacrifices which typified what he was to do and suffer for us. The necessity of these sacrifices proved the necessity of Christ's sacrifice. And God's requiring of them as necessary for redemption, proved also the necessity of our redemption by Christ; and therefore it is evident, that the law pointed out and proved the necessity of our redemption by Christ, and purification by blood."

A Move to London

In 1747 Romaine moved to London "strongly entrenched in notions of his own exalted abilities", but in the capital he was "neither noticed nor applauded". Yet when on the verge of sailing to Hartlepool, with his trunk on board the vessel, he met a total stranger to him, who promised to exert his influence to have Romaine elected to a vacant lectureship at St George's and St Botolph's, Billingsgate. That meeting was surely providential ensuring Romaine's future ministry in London.

It seems that at that time in spite of his intellectual grasp of theology Romaine was not yet converted, or at least did not enjoy the assurance of personal salvation. He gradually grew clearer through reading the Word and through prayer, until in 1749 he reached the crisis point later described by him writing of himself in the third person: "He has been attempting for many years to be something, to do something of himself, but could not succeed; disappointed again and again, yet he could not give it up, till God made him feel, in him, that is, in his flesh dwelled no good thing; and now he writes folly, weakness, sin, on all that is his own; not only clearly convinced that all fullness of good is in Jesus, but is also content that it should be in him."

Previously no lasting fruit from his labours had appeared, though he was erudite and eloquent, but in that same year he began to preach in St Dunstan's in Fleet Street to such great effect that the congregations spilled out into the street. The ministry of the Established Church in London was at a low point, with little true evangelism, but Romaine's bold uncompromising declaration of the Gospel heralded a change for the better. It was desperately needed, for the religious and moral state of the greater part of the populace in London was utterly depraved. Drunkenness, gambling, sexual immorality and corruption were rampant. One of his first converts was a man named John Sanders who later became a state coachman of George III. Sanders heard as he used to say 'to profit'; and received such a deep conviction of sin, and such a terror of the wrath of God due to it, that he was sometimes afraid even to sleep, for fear he would awake in hell.

His Blackfriars Ministry

In 1764 the Rector of the Parishes of St Ann's and St Andrew-by-the-Wardrobe at Blackfriars died. This curious name was derived from its proximity to the King's Great Wardrobe, a building purchased by King Edward III in 1359 to house his state robes. The church had been destroyed in the Great Fire of London but rebuilt by Sir Christopher Wren, the plain brick rectangular building with tower being the last of his city churches. Romaine was still just a curate and lecturer and probably would have remained so had not Lady Huntingdon and other friends exerted themselves to secure that "living" for him. It was typical of Romaine that when he was informed of the efforts being made on his behalf, he declined to canvass the parishioners for their support. In his probation sermon on 2 Corinthians 4.5, "We preach not ourselves, but Christ Jesus the Lord" he stated, "In this ordinance of preaching, and in all our ministerial labours, we are not lords but servants, servants to our great Lord and Master and servants also to you". There was opposition, but Romaine was finally inducted in 1766.

Romaine continued at Blackfriars for the remainder of his life, close to thirty years. J C Ryle wrote of this period: "As rector of a London parish, Romaine became a rallying point for all in London who loved evangelical truth in the Church of England. Man after man, and family after family, gathered around his pulpit, until his congregation became the nucleus of a vast amount of good in the metropolis. His constant, unflinching declaration of Christ's whole truth insensibly produced a powerful impression on men's minds". It became his custom to preach on the first day of each year either on a Hebrew word such as *Shiloh* or *Hosanna* or on a text which he proposed as a motto for that year. In 1794 it was *The God of Hope*, "from whom believers in Christ may hope for all possible good, and to be saved from all possible evil".

Many of his sermons were published, for example *Twelve Discourses upon the Law and the Gospels*, in which he expounded the distinction between the law and the Gospel. Notable among his other published works was the trilogy *The Walk of Faith*, *The Life of Faith*, and the *Triumph of Faith*, the last volume appearing in 1795 shortly before his death. He normally preached four or five times every week and regularly visited the poor and sick of his parish. Time was precious to him as needed for reading, meditation and prayer. Not a moment to be wasted! Worldly pleasure was abhorred! In a rare occurrence he was invited to a house where, after tea, the lady of the house asked him to play cards to which he made no objection. The cards were brought out, and when all were ready to begin playing, Romaine said, "Let us ask the blessing of God." "Ask the blessing of God!" said the lady in great surprise. "I never heard of such a thing before a game of cards." Romaine then enquired, "Ought we to engage in anything on which we cannot ask God's blessing?" This reproof put an end to the card playing - a good lesson on practical sanctification!

Other Aspects of His Ministry

Romaine has been regarded as austere, and certainly he was unbending in his defence of the truth. He has been described as an eighteenth century Puritan, but he was utterly devoted to Christ. When discoursing upon His excellencies it was said that his countenance was illuminated with a majestic and pleasing smile. He published an Essay trenchantly expressing his strict views about hymns, psalms and singing. He urged that only psalms should be sung in church on the ground that nothing should be allowed that threatened the supremacy of Scripture. He opposed the use of church choirs "admired for their fine voices" as being for entertainment, and argued that congregations should stand while singing. His case for this was rather quaintly put: "When subjects go upon any joyful occasion to address their sovereign, is it a custom in any nation of the world to do it sitting? Does the person who pays homage sit, or he who receives it?" He was convinced of the importance of Bible reading and regretted time spent on what he came to regard as the fruitless study of his early years. He declared, "In books I converse with men; in the Bible I converse with God". He advised "Be a Bible student and a Bible Christian."

He enjoyed good health into old age, walking quickly and vigorously right up to the end of his life. His last Sunday evening preaching was on Trinity Sunday 31ˢᵗ May 1795 on 2 Cor 13.14: "The grace of our Lord Jesus Christ be with you all". On 26ᵗʰ July he departed this life in the Triumph of Faith.

JB

Footnote

Much interesting information in '*An Iron Pillar*' *The life and times of William Romaine* by Tim Shelton

CHAPTER 22

John Newton (1725 -1807)

"Amazing Grace…"

The Great Awakening in 18th century England touched a variety of personalities and as in all ages, "the power of God unto salvation" transformed their lives. In terms of outward change the transformation in the life of John Newton was perhaps more dramatic than any other of his time. The story of his conversion remains fascinating more than two hundred years later. It is truly a story of "Amazing Grace", the stirring hymn from Newton's pen that expressed the profound gratitude of this sailor, preacher, pastor and poet. Upon the wall of his study at Olney he painted the text *"And thou shalt remember that thou wast a bondman in the land of Egypt, and the Lord thy God redeemed thee"* (Deut 15.15).

Early Life

John Newton was born in Wapping in 1725, son of a shipmaster. His mother Elizabeth was a godly woman who prayed that her son would become a minister of the Gospel. She died before he was seven years old knowing nothing of the hard and tortuous path his feet would tread before her prayers were answered. His father wished John to follow his footsteps and so he went to sea aged 11 years on board his father's ship making five voyages in the Mediterranean trade. In 1743 he was taken by the Press Gang[1] and put on board HMS *Harwich* a new 50 gun ship. Through his father's influence he was made midshipman but when the ship, bound for the East Indies, called at Plymouth, Newton tried to dessert. He was recaptured, suffered the customary punishment for deserters of flogging, and was demoted to ordinary seaman.

A seaman's life was tough and hard in ways that we can hardly imagine nowadays, but Newton made a hard life even harder for himself. Before being impressed into the Navy he had acquired a book *The Characteristics of Shaftesbury*, the insidious influence of which led him to throw off all restraint. At Madeira he was transferred to another ship, a slaver sailing to Sierra Leone, and among strangers "he could sin without disguise". He later recorded, "From this time I was exceedingly vile, little indeed if anything short of that animated description of an almost irrecoverable state described in 2 Peter 2.14; Having eyes full of adultery, and that cannot cease from sin; beguiling unstable souls".

While on the West African coast he persuaded his captain to let him land on an island where he entered the service of a slave trader. This trader was under the influence of his Negro mistress, who bullied Newton treating him like a slave until he became most pitiable and wretched. However afterwards he gained employment with another trader under less harsh conditions. Newton's father had asked a slave shipmaster to look out for his son, and in 1747 he was picked up by this captain and joined his ship. It was during the voyage back to Britain that the great turning point came in Newton's life. He had been reading Thomas a Kempis just to pass the time, but the thought occurred, "What if these things be true?"

The next day the ship was pitching and rolling through a violent storm and taking in so much water that all hands had to toil at the pumps. Newton said to the captain, "If this will not do, the Lord have mercy upon us", and then he thought, "What mercy can there be for me?" It was the first desire for mercy he had expressed for many years. He began reading the New Testament and found that the scriptures were able to make him wise unto salvation. Thereafter he regarded the day of the storm, 21st March 1748, as a day to be remembered. Eventually the vessel made port in Lough Swilly, and after some repair was carried out, proceeded to Liverpool. Newton stepped ashore no longer an infidel but a Christian. Sadly he did not meet his father who had sailed days before to take up a post as Governor of York Fort in Hudson's Bay where he died in 1750.

Master of a slave ship

It may seem astonishing to us, but Newton continued in the slave trade, sailing as mate in 1748 - 49, and then as master of *Duke of Argyll* followed by two voyages in the *African*. He repressed swearing among his crew and conducted Divine Service, according to the order of the established Church, twice each Lord's Day. The incongruity of a Service being conducted on deck with perhaps two hundred miserable slaves in chains below may be bewildering and awful to us, but it was not to most of his contemporaries. During this period, while at sea, he studied several of the Latin and Greek classics (in which he became self-taught) and read the Bible with increasing devotion. Before taking command of *Duke of Argyll,* Newton had married Mary Catlett at St Margaret's Church, Chatham on 12th February 1750. The Catletts were related to his late mother and he had met Mary when she was thirteen and he was seventeen. Through the wild years that followed he had not forgotten her and early affection blossomed into love. He was a devoted husband in a most happy marriage.

A Better Service

While fitting out another ship in 1754 Newton suffered an unexpected fit and though he recovered he decided to end his seafaring days. In the following year he obtained the position of Surveyor of the Tides at Liverpool in which he continued until his ordination. He carried out his duties conscientiously but became increasingly interested in the Christian ministry, forming friendships with many well known evangelists including Whitefield and Wesley, and gaining the nickname "young Whitefield". He came to the conviction that he should seek ordination for the ministry of the Established Church and in 1758 made his first application. It was unsuccessful because it was expected that all applicants should be learned and have a university education. John Wesley wrote with reference to Newton, "One of eminent learning, as well as unblameable behaviour, cannot be ordained because he was not at the university. What a mere farce is this." Newton persevered, certain that it was the Lord's will, and eventually he was ordained by the Bishop of Lincoln.

Ministry at Olney

In 1764 his ministry commenced in Olney a country town in Buckinghamshire, offering wide scope for his evangelical and pastoral gifts. His strong sense of vocation is apparent from a letter to another minister. "Remember your high calling, you are a minister and ambassador of Christ, you are entrusted with the most honourable and important employment that can engage and animate the heart of man. Filled and fired with a constraining sense of the love of Jesus and the worth of souls; impressed with an ardour to carry the war into Satan's kingdom, to storm his strongholds and rescue his captives, you will have little leisure to think of anything else".

Newton was certainly busy in Olney as his weekly programme demonstrates:[2]

> *Sunday*: 6am Prayer meeting;
>
> Morning, afternoon, and evening - full services with sermon;
>
> 8pm Meeting for prayer and hymn singing in the vicarage
>
> *Monday evening*: Men's Bible class
>
> *Tuesday*: 5am Prayer meeting;
>
> Evening Prayer meeting
>
> *Wednesday*: Classes for young persons and enquirers
>
> *Thursday afternoon*: Children's meeting "to reason with them and to explain the Scriptures in their own little way";
>
> Evening service attended by many from surrounding villages
>
> *Friday evening*: Meeting for members of his society

His pastoral care was also exercised practically. The poor, and those who came a distance, regularly enjoyed the hospitality of the vicarage. John Thornton of Clapham, a wealthy merchant and generous supporter of Christian causes, recognised Newton's power to do good and supported him at the rate of £200 p.a. This was when a curate's stipend was £60 p.a.

In 1766 William Cowper came to reside in the village and their famous friendship began. It was distinguished by their collaboration in writing the Olney Hymns. Newton's best known include *How sweet the name of Jesus sounds* and *Glorious things of Thee are spoken*. In the preface he explained that the hymns were written "to promote the faith and comfort of sincere Christians". They enjoyed sweet fellowship for sixteen fruitful years in Olney.

Ministry at St Mary Woolnoth

In December 1779 he moved to St Mary, Woolnoth in the heart of the City of London where he spent the remainder of his life. Up to that time William Romaine had been the only evangelical parish minister in the city. In a letter written in 1787 Newton recorded "though I was born within about a mile of St Mary, Woolnoth, I had to traverse many thousands, yea scores of thousands of miles before I reached it; but because the Lord was on my side, I passed through numberless dangers by land and sea unhurt, and am still alive to speak of His goodness". His preaching attracted the poor but his personality and experience fitted him to be a spiritual counsellor to people of every stratum of society.

In the years 1784 -1787 he became well acquainted with William Wilberforce and encouraged the younger man to commence his campaign against the slave trade. Newton published a treatise *Reflections on the Slave Trade*, a factual and convincing record which was influential in gathering support for abolition. He wrote, "The ship left the coast with 218 slaves on board. I find by my journal of that voyage (now before me) that we buried 62 on our passage to South Carolina exclusive of those who died before we left the coast." It was an accurate description of conditions on board ships where the slaves were packed "close to each other like books on a shelf". He estimated that the English ships purchased some 60,000 slaves annually along the extent of the coast and that the annual loss of lives could not have been less than 15,000.

Other than his hymns Newton's best literary output was his letters. *Cardiphonia* or *The Utterance of the Heart* published in 1780 became his best known work. The title was suggested to him by Cowper. The book is a collection of 148 letters on spiritual matters written to twenty five correspondents between 1762 and 1780. Newton asked each for permission to publish and all consented – a testimony to his reputation! Around the time of the outbreak of war with France in 1793 he printed *A Letter on Political Debate*. It revealed his attitude towards politics as being first and foremost that of a minister of religion. He was interested most in the spiritual condition of the nation and how it should be viewed in the sight of God. He described his ministerial calling thus: "The Lord has not called me to set nations to right, but to preach the gospel, to proclaim the glory of His name, and to endeavour to win souls."

Mrs Newton died in 1790 and in his latter years Newton was cared for by his niece Eliza. His sight and strength gradually failed but he preached until the last year of his life. He died on 21st December 1807. It was St. Thomas' Day, and one has noted "a fitting day for the aged servant of Christ to pass to his rest". Throughout his ministry he had insisted upon the sin of unbelief and the absolute necessity of belief. The author of *Begone, unbelief ...* may be numbered in a special way among those "that have not seen, and yet have believed".

In the year 1800 it has been estimated that there were over 10,000 clergy in the Church of England. Newton alone among them all had been master of a slave trader. His experiences gave a unique character to his ministry.

His epitaph in St Mary's, written by himself, is as follows –

JOHN NEWTON, Clerk

Once an infidel and libertine

A servant of slaves in Africa,

Was, by the rich mercy of our Lord and Saviour

JESUS CHRIST,

restored, pardoned, and appointed to preach

the Gospel which he had long laboured to destroy,

He ministered,

Near sixteen years in Olney, in Bucks,

And twenty-eight years in this Church

JB

Footnotes

1. The Royal Navy's manning levels in wartime generally exceeded the number of volunteers. Shortfalls were made up by 'press gangs' operating in and around seaports usually under the command of a junior lieutenant; seamen were physically compelled to join the service, a system known as 'impressment'.

2. Much of the information here taken from *The Life and Works of John Newton*, F H Durnford in *Churchman* 56/2, 1942

CHAPTER 23

William Cowper (1731 – 1800)

In His mighty work of grace in the 18th century, God was pleased to use gifted preachers and pious members of the nobility to great spiritual and practical effect. He also used the poetic genius of William Cowper (pronounced "Cooper") to give expression both to Gospel truth and noble Christian sentiment. In the years 1782 to 1837 more than one hundred editions of his poems were published in Britain and almost fifty in America to the great benefit of a wide readership. Perusal of many of the poems enriches the mind and spirit, yet while enjoying the beauty of the verse, a sensitive reader will wonder at the melancholy which often and for so long, clouded this Christian poet's life.

Early Life

The origin of his dark times may be traced to his boyhood. He was born at Great Berkhampstead Rectory on 26th November 1731 becoming the first surviving child of the Rev. John Cowper and his wife Ann. Mrs Cowper was the daughter of Roger Donne of Ludham Hall, Norfolk who was of the same family as John Donne, the famous metaphysical poet of the early 17th century. Cowper was a sensitive child of delicate health, and when only six years old the great misfortune of his life befell him - his mother died after the birth of his brother John. The desolation of his young heart was remembered in the exquisite poem he addressed to her picture, received fifty years later from a cousin.

> *I heard the bell toll'd on thy burial day,*
> *I saw the hearse that bore thee slow away,*
> *And, turning from my nursery window, drew*
> *A long, long sigh, and wept a last adieu!*

Within a year of that sad event he was sent to a school where for two years he suffered cruel bullying. Such a sensitive child would have been the natural target of a bully. Cowper wrote of one of the boys, "I had such a dread of him, that I dare not lift my eyes to his face. I knew him best by his shoe-buckle". When the bullying was discovered he was removed from the school and after an interval was enrolled at Westminster school. Though still very shy and sensitive he became an excellent scholar, and a good cricketer and football player. Among his contemporaries was Warren Hastings later to find fame and fortune in India.

The Kindness of Family and Friends

Upon leaving school in 1748 he was articled for three years to a solicitor, and on completion of his apprenticeship took up residence in Middle Temple being called to the Bar in 1754. It is not known whether he ever had a brief. A relative sought to provide him with an income by nominating him to the post of Clerk of the Journals of the House of Lords. Unfortunately difficulties intervened and he had to face, what was for him, the terrifying prospect of examination at the bar of the House. The prospect deepened existing depression and rendered him incapable of being calmed or consoled even by his brother. He was therefore placed in a lunatic asylum at St Albans owned by Dr Nathaniel Cotton under whose care he slowly recovered his reason.

In 1765 he went to live in Huntingdon to be near his brother at Cambridge, where he became acquainted with a young man named William Unwin, whose parents soon agreed to welcome Cowper as a lodger in their home. It was a most felicitous arrangement and began a period of tranquillity and cheerfulness which ended unexpectedly with the death of Mr Unwin, four days after being thrown from his horse. A short time previously the Unwins had been visited by John Newton who now proposed that the Unwin family, with Cowper, should move to Olney. Mr Unwin had expressed the wish that if his wife survived him Cowper might still dwell with her, and so in September 1767 they came to Olney, initially as guests of the Newtons in the vicarage. Their residence in Olney continued for nineteen years.[1]

Cowper and Newton

A warm bond of fellowship soon developed between Newton and Cowper, yet what an extraordinary contrast they must have presented: John Newton the strong, robust former sailor; William Cowper the delicate, sensitive barrister. The younger man inspired by the ardency of Newton's ministry, visited, read and prayed with the sick, and attended the prayer meetings, even offering extempore prayers – an ordeal for such a shy and private person.

In 1771 at Newton's suggestion Cowper began writing some of the *Olney Hymns* and ultimately contributed sixty-eight to the collection, including the well known and loved *Oh! For a closer walk with God, There is a fountain filled with blood, God moves in a mysterious way* and *Jesus! where'er Thy people meet*. The last named was for use in a small mission room.

The compositions however were interrupted by another period of insanity. His first illness had been full of despair of his own salvation and the same terrible affliction again overwhelmed him. Newton was most tender and loving in his care for the sad, and at times suicidal, patient allowing him to reside for a time in the vicarage. This, with the devoted care of Mrs Unwin, began a slow process of recovery. It is moving to read Cowper's own account of that period. "I was suddenly reduced from my wanted rate of understanding to an almost childish imbecility. I did not lose my senses, but I lost the power to exercise them. I could return a rational answer to a difficult question, but a question was necessary, or I never spoke at all." As he gradually grew better Cowper engaged in gardening and carpentry, with Newton and Mrs Unwin doing their utmost to cheer and sustain him.

His Poetry

Newton left Olney in December 1779 but happily Cowper's progress continued and he resumed his correspondence and occasionally wrote short poems. Mrs Unwin encouraged his endeavours and suggested the *Progress of Error* a moral satire which he tackled enthusiastically. He then wrote *Truth*, *Table Talk* and *Expostulation* in the space of three months! Another two poems followed, *Hope* and *Charity*. Newton submitted the manuscripts to his own publisher who accepted them, with the additional poems *Conversation* and *Retirement*.

These longer poems present arguments of a religious and moral nature. *Conversation* criticises indecent language and noisy wrangling, but extols the pure and undefiled conversation of Christians. The epitome of this is presented in a beautiful devotional passage describing the conversation of the two on the road to Emmaus, of which he writes:

Now theirs was converse such as it behoves
Man to maintain, and such as God approves:
Their views indeed were indistinct and dim,
But yet successful, being aim'd at Him.

The description of the Lord drawing near and speaking to the travellers is equally lovely:

A stranger joined them, courteous as a friend,
And ask'd them, with a kind engaging air,
What their affliction was, and begged a share.
Informed, He gathered up the broken thread,
And, truth and wisdom gracing all He said,
Explain'd, illustrated, and search'd so well
The tender theme on which they chose to dwell,
That reaching home, "The night," they said "is near,
We must not now be parted, sojourn here."

His poem *Truth* contains the well-known lines

Oh, how unlike the complex works of man,
Heaven's easy, artless, unencumbered plan!

Later in the poem Cowper's sense of humour is revealed in his shrewd comparison of a self-righteous Pharisee with a peacock. A reader may well chuckle when reading

The self-applauding bird, the peacock, see –
Mark what a sumptuous Pharisee is he!
Meridian sunbeams tempt him to unfold
His radiant glories, azure, green, and gold:
He treads as if, some solemn music near,
His measured step were govern'd by his ear
And seems to say – "Ye meaner fowl, give place;
I am all splendour, dignity, and grace!"

One day in 1781 when the poet was suffering from a fit of depression a friend, Lady Austen, told him an amusing tale of one named John Gilpin. This delighted Cowper, who spent the night in laughter and wrote *The Diverting History of John Gilpin*, again showing that he could enjoy lighter moments. The same friend persuaded Cowper to try his power at writing blank verse and this led to the remarkable work *The Task*, a long composition in six parts which became immensely popular. Acquaintance with his comic poems led many readers to an appreciation of his more serious work.

The quality of his poetry, and his distinction as a letter writer, has earned him a high place in English literature. He has been ranked among the half-dozen greatest letter writers in the English language. From the Christian standpoint, in addition to the beautiful hymns he wrote, his importance lies in the insight his poetry gives to the character and worth of Christian life, in a form which would last long after the initial excitement of that time of revival had passed.

Latter years

In 1791 Mrs Unwin suffered a paralytic stroke and the effect upon Cowper of her illness and lengthened recovery was very sad. However at times he continued translating Greek and Latin classics and worked on an edition of Milton. After her death he had only glimpses of reason, and his own life closed in melancholy at East Dereham, Norfolk on 25th April 1800.

But let us take our leave of him in happier circumstances. Sitting underneath an ancient oak tree at Yardley Chase, Cowper muses upon the centuries of its existence, and the events of those times. The tree cannot speak, so the poet becomes the oracle and discourses in his own ear of Adam in Eden, possessed of high intelligence, and perfect innocence. He concludes:

He was excused the penalties of dull
Minority. No tutor charged his hand
With the thought-tracing quill or task'd his mind
With problems. History, not wanted yet,
Leaned on her elbow, watching Time, whose course,
Eventful, should supply her with a theme...

We may be sure that Time has now run a large part of its course, and be glad that not only in Old Testament days did poets write, but that also in our later times the genius of Cowper has left a legacy of literature for our enjoyment, and as testimony to Christian grace and virtue.

JB

Footnote

1. Information taken from the Prefatory Memoir contained in *The Poetical Works of William Cowper* published by Chandos Classics

CHAPTER 24

Augustus Montague Toplady
(1740 – 1778)

Among the great torchbearers of the 18th century evangelical awakening considered in these chapters, Augustus Toplady had the shortest life span. He is now mostly remembered as a hymn writer, and particularly as the composer of that masterpiece *Rock of Ages*, but this remarkable man was also an evangelical preacher, a scholar and theologian of no mean reputation who accomplished a great deal in his 38 years.

Early Life and Conversion

Augustus Toplady was born at Farnham in Surrey on 4th November 1740, the only son of Major Richard Toplady who was killed in the siege, by British forces, of Cartagena on the Caribbean coast of present day Colombia in the spring of 1741.[1] Little is known of Toplady's early life other than that he was brought up by his widowed mother who, after her husband's death, had settled at Exeter. At a young age he was sent to Westminster school where he showed considerable ability, and following this he studied at Trinity College Dublin, where he graduated with an MA degree.

In August 1756 he was converted when hearing a layman named James Morris preaching in a barn at Codymain in County Wexford. The text, "But now in Christ Jesus ye who sometimes were far off are made nigh by the blood of Christ" (Eph 2.13), and the preaching founded upon it spoke to the sixteen year old's conscience with great power, and that night he became a new man in Christ Jesus. He later he wrote about the experience, "Strange that I, who had so long sat under the means of grace in England, should be brought nigh to God in an obscure part of Ireland, amidst a handful of God's people met together in a barn, and under the ministry of one who could hardly spell his name! Surely it was the Lord's doing, and is marvellous! The excellency of such power must be of God and cannot be of man. The regenerating Spirit breathes not only on whom, but likewise when, where, and as He listeth".

Ordination

After graduating from Trinity College, Toplady returned to England and was ordained to the ministry of the Church of England. He initially served as curate for short periods at Blagdon in Somerset and Harpford, a small parish near Sidmouth in Devon. An anecdote relating to that period, reveals a conviction that contrasted with the habits of many clergy. "I was buying some books in the spring of 1762, a month or two before I was ordained, from a respectable bookseller. After the business was over, he took me to the furthest end of his long shop and said 'Sir, you will soon be ordained, and I suppose you have not laid in a very great stock of sermons. I can supply you with as many sets as you please, all original, very excellent ones, and they will come for a trifle.' My answer was: 'I certainly shall never be a customer to you in that way; for I am of the opinion that the man who cannot, or will not make his own sermons, is quite unfit to wear the gown. How could you think of my buying ready-made sermons? I would much sooner buy ready-made clothes.' His reply shocked me. 'Nay young gentleman, do not be surprised at my offering you ready-made sermons, for I assure you I have sold ready-made sermons to many a bishop in my time.' My reply was: 'My good sir, if you have any concern for the credit of the Church of England, never tell that news to anybody else hence-forward for ever'." The bookseller must have been astonished. Here was a man of The Book!

Ministry and Preaching

In 1768 Toplady moved to Broad Hembury near Honiton in Devon. Physical weakness would have prevented him from engaging, like Whitefield and the Wesleys, in itinerant open air preaching to thousands of people, but he felt that God had called him to labour in his own rural parish. He declined Lady Huntingdon's request to consider joining her itinerant preachers, replying "and ought I not to see the pillar of divine direction moving before me very visibly and quite incontestably ere I venture to deviate into a more excursive path".

His diary gives an insight into the character of his preaching:

(1) Preach Christ crucified, and dwell chiefly on the blessings resulting from His righteousness, atonement, and intercession.

(2) Avoid all needless controversies in the pulpit except it be when your subject necessarily requires it, or when the truths of God are likely to suffer by your silence.

(3) When you ascend the pulpit, leave your learning behind you; endeavour to preach more to the hearts of your people than to their heads.

(4) Do not affect much oratory. Seek rather to profit than to be admired.

Only ten sermons are included in the collection of his works. One of these was preached at St Anne's Blackfriars (Romaine's church in London) in 1774. He spoke of minds being drawn to high and heavenly things, and continued, "The great business of God's Spirit is to draw up and to bring down – to draw up our affections to Christ, and to bring down the unsearchable riches of grace into our hearts. The knowledge of this, and earnest desires for it, are all the feelings I plead for; and for these feelings I wish ever to plead, satisfied as I am that without some experience and enjoyment of them we can never be happy living or dying".[2]

He lived much alone, seldom going into society and possessing few friends. In childhood he had neither brothers nor sisters, and in manhood he never married. He was engrossed in his ministry, always preaching, visiting parishioners, reading, writing, praying, and spending time in private communion with God. The discipline of study was carried on with unabated zeal, and his wide knowledge and keen intellect made him a formidable opponent in controversy.

In Controversy

The 1770s was a period of sharp contention between some prominent men. John Wesley held the Arminian views which by that time had become prevalent in the Church of England and Augustus Toplady became a leading opponent of Arminianism. In those days views were expressed very robustly, and in his polemical writings Toplady was unsparing of his opponents. He carried the exhortation "rebuke them sharply, that they may be sound in the faith" (Titus 1.13) to an extreme!

Though he was an able and bold defender of Calvinistic views about election, predestination, perseverance, human impotency, and irresistible grace, he did not hold these views as dry theology, believing that the truth must be brought into practical and heartfelt experience. In 1772 he refuted a false implication of the doctrine of election expressed in the phrase, "The elect shall be saved, do what they will". He wrote "The Holy Spirit making the Apostle's pen the channel of unerring inspiration, thus inspired him to write 'According as He (God the Father) hath chosen us in Him (in Christ) before the foundation of the world, that we should (not, 'be saved to do what we will', but) be holy and without blame before Him in love' Eph.1.4. Election is always followed by regeneration; and regeneration is the source of all good works: whence the Apostle adds, in the very next chapter, v.10, 'We (the elect) are His (subsequent) workmanship, created (anew) in Christ Jesus unto good works, which God hath before ordained that we should walk in them.' Consequently it does not follow from the doctrine of absolute predestination that the 'elect shall be saved, do what they will'. On the contrary, they are chosen as much to holiness as to heaven; and are fore-ordained to walk in good works, by virtue of their election from eternity and of their conversion in time".[3]

J C Ryle believed that Toplady's works display extraordinary ability and that his *Historic Proof of the Doctrinal Calvinism of the Church of England* (700 pages) demonstrated a prodigious amount of research and reading. Another writer describes Toplady's historical study of the doctrine of predestination as a valuable contribution to scholarship.[4]

J C Ryle lamented the bitter tone exhibited on both sides of the controversy. He regretted that Toplady seemed to have forgotten the text "in meekness instructing those that oppose themselves" (2 Tim 2.25). But while he could not endorse all the sentiments of Toplady's controversial writings, he claimed for them "the merit of being in principle scriptural, sound, and true". He wrote, "He that only reads Toplady's hymns will find it hard to believe that he could compose his controversial writings. He that only reads his controversial writings will hardly believe that he wrote his hymns".

The Hymn Writer

Yet it may be that the heat of controversy forged conviction of such strength as inspired Toplady to write hymns of the first rank, for though his output was not large, much was of special quality. In *A debtor to mercy alone* he expresses his incalculable debt to the rich mercy of God. The entire hymn firmly rests upon scripture. *Covenant mercy* alludes to the "new covenant" of Hebrews 8. *Nor fear, with Thy righteousness on, my person and offering to bring* relates to the exhortation of Heb10.22. In the second verse, *His promise is Yea and Amen, and never was forfeited yet* immediately reminds one of 2 Cor 1.20. And how could one better express the truth of the believer's eternal security than in the glorious words of verse three -

> *My name from the palms of His hands,*
> *Eternity will not erase;*
> *Impressed on His heart it remains*
> *In marks of indelible grace:*

> *Yes, I to the end shall endure,*
> *As sure as the earnest is given:*
> *More happy, but not more secure,*
> *The souls of the blessed in heaven.*

The verses vibrate with the strong emotion of a man gripped by the truths he writes about. The lines are strong and satisfying. Modern efforts seem rather in the shade!

And what can we say of his classic *Rock of Ages, cleft for me?* Had Toplady only written this one hymn we would still be immensely indebted to him. The entire dependence of a sinner upon divine mercy and grace, and upon the merits of Christ and His saving work is so memorably expressed:

> *Nothing in my hand I bring,*
> *Simply to Thy cross I cling!*
> *Naked, come to Thee for dress;*
> *Helpless, look to Thee for grace;*
> *Foul, I to the fountain fly;*
> *Wash me, Saviour, or I die.*

The writing of this hymn was inspired by him finding shelter in a severe thunderstorm between two massive pillars of rock in Burrington Combe in Somerset. The shelter afforded by that natural refuge turned his mind to his spiritual refuge in the Lord Jesus.[5] The words "everlasting strength" in Isaiah 26.4 may be translated as "a rock of ages".

Last Days

Toplady's health was delicate and in 1775 he was advised to move to London under the impression that the moist air of Broad Hembury was injurious to him. There was little improvement and gradually the insidious disease of tuberculosis, then called consumption, wasted his strength.

Just two months before his death he spoke for the last time in Orange Street Chapel close to Leicester Square. It was a brief exposition of 2 Peter 1.13, "I think it meet, as long as I am in this tabernacle, to stir you up by putting you in remembrance".

His closing days were spent in great peace. A friend wrote, "A short time before his death, I felt his pulse, and he desired to know what I thought of it. I told him that his heart evidently beat almost every day weaker and weaker. He replied immediately, with the sweetest smile on his countenance, 'Why that is a good sign that my death is fast approaching, and blessed be God, I can add that my heart beats every day stronger and stronger for glory'." He quietly fell asleep in Jesus on 11th August 1778, and was buried in Tottenham Court Chapel in the presence of thousands of people from all parts of London and beyond.

J C Ryle offered this assessment of Toplady's life: "I firmly believe that he was a good man, and a great man, and did a work for Christ which will never be overthrown. He will stand in his lot at the last day in a high place, when many, perhaps whom the world liked better shall be put to shame".

JB

Footnotes

1. The siege and battle of Cartagena occurred during the so called *War of Jenkin's Ear*. The Royal Navy and British Army launched a major attack on Cartagena which was repulsed by the defending Spanish force. The British forces suffered enormous casualties though more died from disease, especially yellow fever, than were killed in action.

2. This and other quotations of J C Ryle are from his *Toplady and His Ministry* taken from *Christian Leaders of the 18th Century.*

3. *Toplady on Predestination* Cecil Proctor in Churchman 077/1, 1963

4. Ibid

5. *Hymns and Their Writers* by Jack Strahan, Gospel Tract Publications, 1989

CHAPTER 25

Henry Venn (1724 – 1797)

The life story of Henry Venn shows how an earnest, upright, young clergyman discovered that it is, "not of works of righteousness that we have done, but according to his mercy he saved us, by the washing of regenerating, and renewing of the Holy Ghost" (Titus 3.5). His conversion led to a valuable ministry during the time of the Evangelical Awakening.

Henry Venn was born on 2nd March 1724 at Barnes in Surrey. His father Richard Venn was a High Church minister, "exemplary and learned", and "very zealous for the interests of the Church of England". The family could trace an unbroken line of clergy stretching back to the Reformation period.

Education and Ordination

With such a family history it not surprising that Henry followed in his father's footsteps. He went up to Jesus College Cambridge in 1742 where he was quickly admitted to a wide circle of friends, men who had known his father and his elder brother. By all accounts he was of equable temper, and of a cheerful and friendly disposition. He was also of high moral character. He graduated with an MA degree in 1747 when, there being no fellowship vacant in his own college, he was unanimously elected a fellow of Queen's, in which he continued until his marriage in 1757.

Venn was an excellent cricketer, one of the best in the university. In the week before his ordination he played in a match between Surrey and All England. When the game was over he threw down his bat and said, "Whoever wants a bat, which has done me good service, may take that; as I have no further occasion for it." His astonished friends asked why. He answered, "Because I am to be ordained on Sunday, and I will never have it said of me, 'Well struck Parson!' " He never went back on that resolve.

Conversion

For a brief period he held a curacy at Barton Cambridgeshire, before moving to West Horsley, Surrey. Venn was clearly a most sincere and conscientious young man who wished to carry out his duties faithfully. The problem was, he had no heart experience of salvation. Like the Wesleys, Whitefield, Grimshaw and others he went through a time of striving to please God by prayer, fasting and religious devotions, and like them he suffered disappointment. A deep impression was made upon his mind by a form of prayer he frequently used, "that I may live to the glory of Thy name". He would ask himself, "What is it to live to the glory of God? Do I live as I pray?" Reading William Law's *A Serious Call to a Devout and Holy Life* deepened his concerns, but provided no answer, as it did not point to the saving work of Christ.

As he concentrated more on reading Scripture, he began to question aspects of Law's theology, and as he did, sometime during 1752-53 he discovered "the particular provision that is made for fallen man in the Gospel of our blessed Lord and Saviour Jesus Christ". Until then his religion had been "a hard service". Now "the religion of Christ became a religion of hope, and peace, and joy". He saw that our sins are taken away by the blood of Christ, and that, being justified by faith in Him, we have peace with God through our Lord Jesus Christ. He saw with wonder the infinite tenderness, compassion, and love of the Saviour, upon whom he now relied.[1] He had the same desire for holiness, but now from a different motive.

Curate at Clapham

In 1754 Venn became curate at Clapham, then a village outside of London, where he continued for five years. Four times each week he rode into London to lecture in three churches, so that in a given week he would preach six times. During this period he met Thomas Haweis, George Whitefield and Lady Huntingdon, all of whom helped him to reach enjoyment of full deliverance, and to remove the lingering effects of mystical writers upon his thinking and ministry.

Venn, with Whitefield and Martin Madan, had visited the Countess at her home at Clifton near Bristol. Afterwards with considerable perspicuity she wrote to Venn, "O, my friend! We can make no atonement to a violated law – we have no inward holiness of our own; the Lord Jesus Christ is the Lord our Righteousness. Cling not to such beggarly elements, such filthy rags – mere cobwebs of Pharasaical pride – but look to Him who hath wrought out a perfect righteousness for His people. Preach Christ crucified as the only foundation of the sinner's hope. Preach Him as the Author and Finisher, as well as the sole object of faith – that faith which is the gift of God. Exhort Christless impenitent sinners to fly to this city of refuge – to look to Him who is exalted as Prince and Saviour, to give repentance and the remission of sins. Go on thus, and may your bow abide in strength!" Such a letter must have been encouraging to Venn in completing his journey from High Church to clear evangelical ground. It gives an insight into the Countess's grasp of Christian doctrine, and why she was so respected by the men of the Great Awakening.

Marriage

Henry Venn's evangelical convictions were further strengthened by his marriage in 1757 to Miss Eling Bishop from Ipswich. She was a minister's daughter and proved to be a spiritual help meet for Venn. He and Eling – known as Mira – were devoted to each other. Their five children were raised in a most happy home where daily family worship was regarded as essential to their education and upbringing. It was a terrible blow to Venn when she died in 1767. He wrote to Lady Huntingdon, "Did I not know the Lord to be mine into what a deplorable condition should I have been now cast. I have lost her when her industry, and ingenuity and tender love and care of her children were all beginning to be perceived by the two older girls. I have lost her when her soul was as a watered garden, when her mouth was opened to speak for God. Nevertheless I can say All is well! Hallelujah for the Lord God omnipotent reigneth."

Preacher at Huddersfield

In 1759 the family moved from Clapham to Huddersfield where for twelve years Venn exercised a fruitful ministry which brought about a remarkable moral and spiritual transformation in the town. His first sermon was on the text "my heart's desire and prayer to God for Israel is that they might be saved". Shortly before, John Wesley had called men and women he was preaching to, "the wildest congregation I have seen in Yorkshire". He soon became acquainted with William Grimshaw (see Chapter 19), as Haworth was little more than twenty miles away. Their friendship left an indelible mark on Venn, and his ministry resembled the older man's in many respects. Travelling through the surrounding countryside on horseback, visiting parishioners in lonely farms and cottages, he preached in barns, private homes or wherever people gathered. He drew the same large congregations, so that very often the church was too small and the preaching had to be in the open air.

In 1824 his grandson Henry Venn visited Huddersfield and spoke to old people who remembered the days of his grandfather's ministry. One, William Brook, was sixteen when he went with his uncle to Church on a Thursday evening. A great crowd was within the church, all silent, many weeping. The text was "Thou art weighed in the balances, and art found wanting". They left together, and after walking some distance in silence, the uncle stood with his back to a wall and burst into tears saying, "I can't stand this", his conviction of sin was so powerful. He was saved and became a changed man. Brook said, "I was not so much affected at that time; but I could not, after that sermon, be easy in sin; and I began to pray regularly; and so, by degrees, I was brought to know myself, and seek salvation in earnest".[2]

Busy though he was, Venn also travelled to preach at the

request of Lady Huntingdon. One such place was Ote Hall, a stately home about 10 miles from Brighton, where in 1761 the great hall was turned into a place for preaching. One day a man known locally as 'Old Abraham' a veteran of the battlefields of Europe, now nearly one hundred years old, came in. As Venn concluded his preaching the old soldier turned to the one sitting next to him and said, "Ah, neighbour, this is the very truth of the word of God that I have been seeking for, and never heard it so plain before." For six more years 'Old Abraham' was spared to grow in grace, his snow white hair making him a conspicuous member of the congregation.[3]

Through his pen, Venn's influence reached far beyond the places where he preached. His *Complete Duty of Man*, a devotional and practical book was published in 1763. He addressed issues of everyday life in a wholly different way to *The Whole Duty of Man* published in the previous century in reaction to Puritan thought and practise, and chained in churches for people to read. Evangelicals had often protested against it but Venn provided a substitute. He wrote "All treatises to promote holiness must be deplorably defective, unless the Cross of Christ be laid as the foundation, constantly kept in view, and every duty enforced as having relation to the Redeemer".

Pastor at Yelling

Strenuous labours took their toll upon his health and he felt unable to continue at Huddersfield. In 1771 he moved to his final charge at Yelling, twelve miles from Cambridge. Soon after this he married again. His second wife was a widow, and again, the daughter of a minister. His last phase of service had rich pastoral value through which his spiritual influence spread to younger men who could bear the torch, and communicate the vibrancy of the mid-century awakening to others.

A notable example was in his friendship with Charles Simeon, vicar of Holy Trinity Church, Cambridge, and a mentor of many students. Simeon learned from the ardour and zeal of Venn and came to regard him as his spiritual father. Another instance relates to his son John who served as rector of Holy Trinity Church at Clapham from 1792 to 1813. John Venn was highly respected by William Wilberforce, Henry Thornton, Zachary Macaulay, and the others who were known as the Clapham Sect or Saints. These men became renowned for their influence for social change and the furtherance of missionary endeavour. John Venn presided at the organising meeting of the Church Missionary Society in 1799.

Venn also communicated his pastoral care in correspondence with many who sought his help. His letters imparted sage counsel and advice, and reveal a joyful man of deep spirituality with an unwavering love for God. A selection of 200 letters was later published by his grandson (see Footnote 1).

His legacy

The influence of Henry Venn continued through his grandchildren. His eldest daughter Eling married Charles Elliot of Brighton in 1785. Their daughter Charlotte (1789 – 1871) wrote the well-known hymn *Just as I am without one plea, but that Thy blood was shed for me*. His grandson Henry was Honorary Secretary of the Church Missionary Society from 1841 to 1873. The term "honorary" did not mean for him a passive role. He was dedicated and active in promoting foreign missions. He advocated the encouragement of native ministry and has been remembered as the father of the "three selfs" formula: self-supporting, self-governing, and self-propagating.

After suffering a stroke in December 1796 Mr Venn went to live with his son John in Clapham, from where he entered into the joy of his Lord on 24th June 1797.

JB

Footnotes

1. Much of this account taken from *The Life and a Selection from the letters of the late Rev. Henry Venn, MA,* 1834 by John Venn (son) edited by Henry Venn (grandson), re-published by Banner of Truth Edinburgh, 1993.

2. Ibid

3. *Selina Countess of Huntingdon* by Faith Cook, page 196

CHAPTER 26

Thomas Haweis (1734 – 1820)

Many modern travellers would still consider a journey from Aberdeen to Cornwall long and tedious whether driving on motorways, or 'letting the train take the strain'. Disruptions or delays even of a few hours often result in howls of protest, which simply shows how cosseted and molly coddled many have become in the western world!

About three hundred years ago, such a journey really was a serious and lengthy undertaking, and not without its dangers. But our forefathers were hardy souls, and sometime, probably during the 1720s, a Scotsman named George Conan journeyed from Aberdeen to Truro to take up the position of Master in the Grammar School. It was to be an eventful appointment, for Conan, described as a "scholar and a saint", was instrumental in the conversion of Samuel Walker, curate to an absentee vicar of St Mary's Church in Truro, and became a link in the chain leading to the salvation of Thomas Haweis and Thomas Wills both unsung heroes of the 18th century revival.

School and University

Haweis was born in 1732[1] in Redruth where his father practised as a solicitor. He was of good Cornish stock, his father Thomas hailing from Penzance, and his mother from Falmouth. His surname was pronounced 'Haws', Thomas in later life rhyming it in a comic verse with 'paws'. He became a scholar at Truro Grammar School during Conan's time as Master, where he benefited not only from a good classical education, but more importantly from the evangelical influence of both Conan and

Walker, which led directly to his conversion. His family could not afford to send him to university, so after leaving school he was apprenticed to an apothecary. Later he was sponsored to enter Christ's College Oxford, where he gathered other students together in a prayer group viewed by many as a second "Holy Club".

Ordination at Oxford

In 1757 he was ordained as curate at St Mary Magdalene in Oxford. In that same year a young student from Truro entered Magdalen Hall, Thomas Wills who also had been taught by George Conan at Truro Grammar School, and been under the ministry of Samuel Walker. Haweis took Wills under his wing, and God used the influence of the small praying group at the university to bring the young man into the assurance of salvation. Thomas Wills became a noted preacher who exercised a fruitful ministry in his home town for ten years. He later married a niece of the Countess of Huntingdon[2]. He possessed, "a grand majestic voice that commanded attention," and used it well when, "proclaiming to thousands the grand, important, and essential truths of the Gospel".[3]

Another incident of the time reveals Haweis' capacity as a spiritual guide. During a visit to London he formed a close acquaintance with Henry Venn (previous chapter). In the course of a discussion on the issue of Calvinism as opposed to Arminianism, Haweis discoursed upon God's sovereign control in the affairs of men. Venn exclaimed, "Allow me, my dear Haweis, to be something more than a stone!" Gradually however Venn began to understand the truths being explained to him, and Haweis later commented, "He very shortly after learned that it was of stones that God raised up children unto Abraham, and that it is His grace alone which takes away the heart of stone and gives a heart of flesh".[4]

During Haweis' time at St Mary Magdalene opposition to plain Gospel preaching in Oxford was growing, and in 1762 he was dismissed from his curacy for no other offence than that his fearless and uncompromising preaching was attracting ever increasing congregations. Serious opposition to evangelical influence in the university broke out into the open in an infamous case in 1768. Seven students, after a formal trial (described as a travesty of justice) before the Vice-Chancellor of the university, were expelled from St Edmund Hall. They were described as 'enthusiasts who talked of regeneration, inspiration and drawing nigh unto God'.

Lock Hospital

Following his time at Oxford, Haweis went to London. He was given hospitality in the home of Martin Madan who appointed him an assistant chaplain at the Lock Hospital, situated in the present day Grosvenor Square near Hyde Park. The hospital, where doctors gave their service gratis, had been founded in 1746 to be a refuge for fallen and destitute women, where moral and spiritual, as well as medical help could be provided. Haweis helped Madan to compile a hymn book for use in the chapel.

Madan's history is interesting and unusual. He had trained as a lawyer and had been called to the Bar in 1748. One evening in a coffee house he was persuaded to go to hear John Wesley preaching so that afterward he could use his talent of mimicry to amuse his friends. In the chapel Wesley announced his text, "Prepare to meet thy God" with such solemnity that Madan was compelled to listen and the Word of God penetrated his heart. Afterwards his friends asked, "if he had taken off the old Methodist". He replied, "No, he has taken me off."

From that night he forsook their company and determined to prepare himself for Christian service. In 1750 he began to preach at the chapel adjoining the Lock Hospital. He was well learned in the original languages of Scripture, and became an impressive preacher.[5] In 1780 however Madan published a very controversial work, *Thelyphtora* in which he advocated polygamy (basing this on certain Old Testament passages e.g. Deut 22.28 -29) as a means addressing the problems of women who had been seduced. It aroused a storm of indignant protest, and Haweis' former association with Madan did not deter him from publishing a rebuttal in his *A Scriptural Refutation of the Arguments for Polygamy.*

Rector of Aldwinkle

In 1764 George Whitefield, evidently impressed by Haweis' abilities, encouraged him to go to America to take up a ministry in Philadelphia; however he declined, deciding instead to accept the preferment as Rector of All Saints, Aldwinkle, in Northamptonshire, which position he retained until his death. Around this time Haweis became known to the Countess of Huntingdon (Ch 18). He soon gained her confidence and was regularly asked to preach in many of her chapels. She appointed him as one of her private chaplains in 1774. When the commodious Spa Fields Chapel at Clerkenwell in North London was re-opened in March 1779 after being leased by the Countess, Haweis preached on the first day. He set the tone for the future ministry at Spa Fields by his address on *We preach Christ crucified.*

Haweis soon found himself in difficulties, falling foul of the ecclesiastical laws of the Established Church. The obduracy of the local curate led him to commence legal proceedings, challenging the right of Haweis and others to preach in his parish. The verdict of the Bishop of London's Consistory Court, in spite of a petition from many local residents, was against Haweis and his colleagues. It was the precedent set by that verdict that forced the Countess to protect all her chapels under the 1689 Toleration Act by registering them as Dissenting Meeting Rooms, leading to the formation of the Huntingdon Connexion.

A wider evangelism

In spite of all this, Haweis retained his strong attachment to the Established Church, its ordinances and liturgy. He firmly believed that the mission of the church was to preach the Gospel. Unfortunately many of the hierarchy had no more sense of that mission then, than their successors do now. For some time Haweis felt unable to preach for the Countess in her chapels because of their Dissenting status; however later his association with her work resumed and he preached at Bath and in other chapels, balancing an itinerant ministry with his parish responsibilities at Aldwinkle. Following the death of Lady Huntingdon in 1791 he was surprised to discover that she had left the Trusteeship of the Connexion to him, his second wife Jenetta Orton, and two others. Deeply anxious about the difficulties he might face in this position he sought advice from William Romaine, who like himself was a strong churchman. Romaine's clear advice was to accept, adding that he would do so were he in the same situation. Haweis thereafter undertook responsibility to organise supply for the many pulpits and preaching points throughout the country although in doing so he sought to ensure that the Connexion kept as close to the Church of England as was possible.

Missionary Interests

Haweis was also active in promoting overseas missions with a particular interest in the South Seas, as the islands of the South Pacific were then known. Penal colonies had been recently established in Australia and more voyages were being made across the vast Pacific Ocean as trade was developing with various island groups. Some contacts between Europeans and native populations had unhappy consequences, but Haweis and others longed to bring the Gospel to dispel the darkness of heathendom and ameliorate the ravages of disease and alcohol among the natives.

In 1791 he was active in preparations to send two missionaries, Michael Waugh and John Price, former students at Travecca College, to the South Seas. He took steps to secure passage for them on board HMS *Providence*[6] under the command of Captain William Bligh of HMS *Bounty* fame. His efforts failed when Waugh and Price insisted upon being ordained before departure and Episcopal ordination was refused by the Bishop of London, and by the Archbishop of Canterbury. This disappointment did not dampen his interest and at meetings held in September 1795 for the inauguration of the London Missionary Society, he preached on "Go ye into all the world, and preach the gospel to every creature" (Mark 16.15). Perhaps due to his influence Tahiti became the first field of labour to which the Society sent missionaries.

Hymns and other writing

Thomas Haweis wrote a good number of hymns, some of considerable merit. *Lord Jesus to tell of Thy love / Our souls would for ever delight* is sung and enjoyed to this day; another *Behold the Lamb! 'Tis He who bore / Sin's burden on the tree* is included in *Hymns of Light and Love*. He also wrote a number of prose works including his 3 volume *Impartial and Succinct History of the Rise, Declension and Revival of the Church of Christ* which includes a brief account of Lady Huntingdon's life work with many interesting details of her early life, and *The Evangelical Expositor; or a Commentary on the Holy Bible*. His *Evangelical Principles and Practice* was a collection of fourteen of his sermons and formed part of the training material for students preparing for the ministry in the Countess of Huntingdon Connexion. Haweis being a great admirer of William Romaine, wrote *The Life of William Romaine* in 1797.

Personal life

On 3rd January 1771 he married a widow, Judith Wordsworth nee Townsend, a lady who much enjoyed the study of Hebrew. Their marriage was short as Judith died tragically in 1786 after she was thrown from a cart. Two years later he married Jenetta Orton who had been converted through his preaching. She had been a personal companion and helper of Lady Huntington. He was bereaved again when Jenetta died in 1799, but in 1802 he married Elizabeth (Bessie) McDowall who survived him.

Being younger than many of the prominent figures of the 18th century revival, his own long life meant that he outlived them all. For the twenty years he lived into the 19th century he must have been viewed as a living link to a former era, and with celebrated servants of God.

He died on 11th February 1820 and was buried at Bath Abbey.

JB

Footnotes

1. There is a question over the year of his birth. Most sources give it as 1734, but John Julian in his *Dictionary of Hymnology* gives 1732. This fits better with some later dates.

2. From *Selina Countess of Huntingdon* by Faith Cook, page 361

3. Ibid, page 384

4. Ibid, page 163

5. From *An Iron Pillar, the life and times of William Romaine* by Tim Shenton

6. Bligh was one of the few examples of a commissioned officer who "came up through the hawse pipe". He had joined the navy as a boy, served as an able seaman, and sailed with Captain James Cook. *Providence* was a sloop of war, 107ft 4ins overall length. Small ships sailed on very long voyages in those days.

CHAPTER 27

Robert Haldane (1764 – 1842)

The lives and labours of many evangelists during the 18th century have been the subject of earlier chapters. England was greatly privileged by their preaching. It was much less so in Scotland, although visits such as that by Whitefield to Glasgow and Cambuslang in 1741 (see Ch 17) brought great blessing. Within the Church of Scotland a few ministers were "holding forth the word of life" within their parishes, but more generally the land was shrouded in darkness, dark as midnight! One faithful Church of Scotland minister wrote of many of the clergy that, "they seemed miserable in the discharge of every ministerial duty. To deliver a Gospel sermon or preach to the hearts and consciences of dying sinners was as completely beyond them as to speak in the language of angels".[1]

Beginnings of revival

Before the century ended however a fresh blaze of "the light of the glorious gospel" was breaking out. Two brothers, Robert and James Haldane had been converted, and had become instruments in the Lord's hand for revival in Scotland. Haldanes had been active at crucial times in Scotland's history. Sir John Haldane fell on the fatal field of Flodden; another John was one of the Members for the county of Perth in the last Scottish parliament, and the first Member for that county in the British House of Commons. But it would be Robert and James Haldane who would do the family's most worthwhile work in Scotland in the period between the awakening of the 18th century and the great revivals of the 19th century.

The Haldane family

The Haldane family of Gleneagles descended from Roger de Halden who was granted a charter of the lands of Gleneagles by King William the Lyon in the 12th century. Much later several of the family became seafarers among whom Robert Haldane (grandfather of Robert and James) became the first Scotsman to command an East India Company ship.

When Captain Haldane died without surviving issue, his estate was divided. Airthrey near Stirling was bequeathed to his nephew James Haldane and Gleneagles to another nephew. This James Haldane had married a first cousin, Katherine, daughter of Alexander Duncan and Helen Haldane. They had three children, Robert born in 1764 in London, Helen, born in 1765, and James born in 1768 in Dundee, a fortnight after his father's death. Their widowed mother Katherine[2] instilled a sense of the importance of eternity into her children's minds, and impressed upon them the necessity of prayer. She taught them to memorise Psalms, other portions of Scripture and the Shorter Catechism.[3] On her death in 1774 the orphaned children were left in the care of their grandmother and their uncle. Both sons later testified to the spiritual value of their saintly mother's training which bore fruit in their lives many years afterwards.

Midshipman Haldane

The boys had a good education at Edinburgh High School before going to sea. Robert entered Royal Naval service in 1780 on board *Monarch* a 74 gun ship of the line commanded by his uncle. The following year he joined the 80 gun ship *Foudroyant* (she had retained her French name after capture). His captain was now Sir John Jervis who later became Earl St.Vincent after his famous victory over a much larger Spanish fleet off Cape St Vincent in February 1797. Robert saw action in *Foudroyant* in which as a midshipman he had charge of a number of guns, but the end of the American Revolutionary wars in 1783 brought his short naval career to a close. After a period of study at Edinburgh University, Robert married in

1786 and settled into the estate of Airthrey inherited from his father.

A Country Gentleman

Robert now enjoyed the life of a country gentleman, developing his estate with little interest in the wider world, but like many others his insularity was disturbed by the impact of the French Revolution. He became interested in philosophical and political debate, but God was dealing with him and he discovered that the speculations and ideas of men could not secure a better order for mankind. Referring to this period of his interest in politics he recalled, "I eagerly caught at them as a pleasing speculation. As a fleeting phantom they eluded my grasp; but missing the shadow I caught the substance and while obliged to abandon these confessedly empty and unsatisfactory pursuits, I obtained in some measure the solid consolations of the Gospel".

Conversion

In his religious life he had been contenting himself with "a common and worthless profession". He wrote, "I endeavoured to be decent, and what is called moral, but was ignorant of my lost state by nature as well as of the strictness, purity and extent of the Divine law. While I spoke of a Saviour I was little acquainted with His character, the value of His sufferings and death, or the need I stood in of the atoning efficacy of His pardoning blood, so that I may say as Paul, concerning the Gentiles of old, 'He was found of me who sought him not' ". With conscience awakened he conversed with several clergymen, but the person from whom he derived real spiritual help was a stone-mason then working on the estate. This man was an intelligent and well taught Christian who was able to unfold the Gospel to Mr Haldane. Ever after he looked back with thankfulness to the time spent with that humble man. His conversion was "neither sudden nor violent but it was the act of God and as such, mysterious in its origin, decisive in its character, and effectual in its results".[4] With characteristic energy and zeal he applied himself to the study of the Bible, and quickly became committed to the spread of the Gospel.

Called to Serve

Sometime later a friend gave him a copy of the first of the periodical accounts of the Baptist Mission founded by Dr William Carey at Serampore on the River Hooghly in India. This report made an indelible impression upon him and he was one of the first in Scotland to be a member of the recently founded London Missionary Society. His mind became much occupied with missionary work, and after prayerful consideration he proposed to fund and lead a mission to Benares. This city was within the territory administered by the East India Company, so he sought the permission of the British Government, and of the Company's Court of Directors. Permission was firmly refused, one of the directors stating that "he would rather see a band of devils in India than a band of missionaries". Ultimately Haldane recognised that the Lord had not opened the door.

A large part of the estate at Airthrey was sold in 1798. Funds ear-marked to finance the intended Bengal Mission were now devoted to Home Missions and the formation in that year of the "Society for Propagating the Gospel at Home". He was closely involved with the purchase of buildings in Edinburgh, Glasgow and Dundee to become Tabernacles after the model of Whitefield's in London. The Edinburgh Tabernacle built on Leith Walk with seating for 3,200, was opened in May 1801.

A Visit to the Continent

He had cherished a desire to visit the Continent with the Gospel and did so after the war with France ended. In 1816 he and his wife left Scotland to travel, first to Paris, and then to Geneva. He found nothing to encourage in that place which had been a citadel of the Reformation. He continued on through Switzerland but after some hesitation resolved to return to Geneva, where providentially, he met a young student of theology who was instrumental in introducing fellow students to Mr Haldane. Soon over twenty of them were being instructed in Gospel truth. M Monod later recalled "We were most of us thoughtless, deeply tainted with worldliness, and immersed in gaiety. Though students of theology, true theology was one of the things of which we knew the least. I still see in my mind's eye his tall and manly figure, his English Bible in his hand, wielding as his only weapon that Word which is the sword of the Spirit; satisfying every objection, removing every difficulty, answering every question by a prompt reference to various passages".

The studies were in the Epistle to the Romans and led to a recovery of the truth amongst the Protestants of Switzerland and France. A notable convert was Dr Merle D' Aubigne the celebrated historian of the Reformation. In a speech in Edinburgh in 1845 he declared, "If Geneva gave something to Scotland at the time of the Reformation, if she communicated light to John Knox, Geneva has received something from Scotland in return, in the blessed exertions of Robert Haldane".[5]

A Written Ministry

Haldane became deeply interested in the Romans epistle, and the fruit of careful study over thirty years was his *Exposition of the Epistle to the Romans* published in three volumes, the first appearing in 1835, the second in 1837, the third in 1839. Dr Thomas Chalmers[6] called it "a well-built commentary", and recommended it to students of theology. For himself he found it "solid and congenial food".

Haldane's reputation as a writer had been established by his *Evidence and Authority of Divine Revelation* published in 1816. He felt that such evidences ought to be studied by Christians, not because they doubt, but because they desire to know more of the certainty of those things, which they most surely believe. An enlarged and improved edition appeared in 1834. Its content and style were relevant to its time in combating the influence of the teachings of such as David Hume the Scottish moral philosopher.

Preaching and Teaching

Though Robert Haldane did not itinerate he preached regularly. His first sermon had been delivered in April 1798 in a barn near Taymouth where he expounded Ephesians 2.1-8. When he lived at Auchingray, between Edinburgh and Glasgow, it was his custom each Lord's Day to ride more than six miles to Airdrie to minister. He followed the practice of those days by combining two services into one, lasting from noon to 3 pm, his two sermons separated by a psalm, prayer and a second psalm. In notes made of one sermon he made an interesting reference to two difficulties. The first he stated was "to convince a man that he is a sinner", the second, "to persuade a believer that he is forever safe in Christ".

He remained vigorous into old age but in 1841 his strength began to decline. In 1842, though largely confined to his home in Edinburgh, he remained busy in various matters including writing tracts. From August he became more feeble until on Monday 12th December he quietly departed to be with Christ. The last words he was heard to utter were, "For ever with the Lord". His wife survived him for exactly six months. Robert Haldane must have been greatly missed by his younger brother. A gentleman once seeing them together exclaimed, "There they are! The two brothers, they have always dwelt together in unity".

JB

Footnotes

1. From *Autobiography of Dr Hamilton of Strathblane*

2. Katherine's brother Admiral Lord Duncan of Dundee won a crushing victory over the Dutch fleet at the battle of Camperdown in October 1797.

3. From *The Lives of Robert and James Haldane* published 1852, and by Banner of Truth 1990

4. Ibid, page 92

5. Ibid, quotations from pages 430 and 431

6. Chalmers was born in Anstruther, Fife in 1780. A staunch evangelical he was the first Moderator of the Free Church of Scotland following the Disruption in the Church of Scotland in 1843.

CHAPTER 28

James Haldane (1768 – 1851)

When Robert Haldane's brother James went to sea he followed in his father's footsteps. His intended career was in the service of the Honourable East India Company, and when sixteen he sailed as a midshipman on the *Duke of Montrose* bound for Bombay and China. The Company then enjoyed a monopoly of the trade to India and the East. The ships were heavily manned and run man o' war fashion, making slow passages with calls at various ports en-route. For three generations the Haldane family had held substantial interests in ships chartered by the Company so that a very lucrative career beckoned to young James. He quickly adapted to shipboard life, becoming a smart and energetic seaman while studying to master navigation skills. Further voyages were on different ships but for his fourth voyage he was appointed second officer of his first ship *Duke of Montrose*.

Marriage and Conversion

The voyage ended in June 1793 and James returned to his brother's house at Airthrey where he met a young lady whom he married in September. Mary Joass was the only daughter of Major Alexander Joass from Banffshire. Shortly afterwards James was appointed captain of the *Melville Castle* which was to sail in convoy from Portsmouth in December.[1] A very lengthy delay however ensued, and while the ship lay at anchor at Spithead, Haldane began to read his Bible with greater earnestness than for many years. God began a work of grace in his soul and he resigned his post on *Melville Castle*, and returned to Scotland. Talking to various ministers he found many had embraced Socinian views and were rationalists denying much of the truth of Divine revelation,[2] however the knowledge of Scripture acquired in early life, preserved him from their evil influence and at length he gained the assurance of salvation.

His seagoing career over, he expected to live a quiet and unambitious life. The Lord however had a much greater plan for him. While residing in Edinburgh he became acquainted with two active and devoted laymen, John Campbell and John Aikman. Mr Campbell owned a large ironmonger's shop in the Grassmarket and his warehouse was the only repository in Edinburgh for Christian periodicals and tracts. He was a model city missioner, a Sunday School teacher, Scripture reader and tract distributor. It was in his shop that James Haldane met Aikman who had relinquished a lucrative business in Jamaica after having been brought to Christ through reading John Newton's *Cardiphonia,* or *The Utterance of the Heart.* Aikman's health had suffered from living in the tropics but he was then attending Divinity lectures with a view to the ministry. Fellowship with these men stimulated James Haldane's spiritual growth and soon he shared their desires for the spread of the Gospel.

Apathy and Indifference in the Church

Zealous men with a passion for souls were sorely needed to awaken the people of Scotland from their "sleep of death". The notorious General Assembly of the Church of Scotland of 1796[3] had rejected the Resolution "That it is the duty of Christians to carry the Gospel to the heathen world". One so called "moderate" minister had stated in the debate, "Men must be polished and refined in their manners before they can be properly enlightened in religious truths". Another questioned "Why send missionaries to foreign parts, when there is so much ignorance, unbelief and immorality at your own doors?"

A Great Door and Effectual

Sometime after this Assembly debate, a friend of Mr Campbell told him of the need of the people of Gilmerton, a large mining village near Edinburgh, who he said "had heard nothing like the Gospel in the Parish Church for at least forty years". A preacher named Joseph Rate from Gosport visited Edinburgh at that time and Campbell asked him to preach at Gilmerton, which he consented to do. The following Sunday evening James Haldane and John Aikman walked to Gilmerton with Mr Rate to find a house full of people waiting for them. The second Sunday the number increased, but during that week Mr Rate had to leave Edinburgh and Haldane proposed that if Aikman would preach on the next Sunday then he would do so on the one following. Thus it came to pass that James Haldane preached for the first time on 6th May 1797. The preaching at Gilmerton was attended by blessing and many came to hear Mr Aikman and the Sea Captain. The parish minister tried to stop the meetings by contriving to deprive them of the school-house but a spacious loft, then a large barn were procured, in which crowds heard plain, pointed Gospel preaching.[4] Many, even some evangelical clergy, had serious misgivings about laymen preaching, but the Lord put His seal of approval upon the work at Gilmerton, and then upon the first lengthy itinerary over the North of Scotland later in the same year.

Northwards with the Gospel

When James Haldane and John Aikman commenced their first tour, they took their commission from the Bible "Go ye into all the world and preach the Gospel". Leaving Edinburgh on 12th July 1797 they travelled north preaching at Perth, Scone, Coupar Angus and Kirriemuir. Then it was on to Forfar and Brechin, where the town drummer assisted by announcing the sermon. They preached at Montrose, Bervie and Stonehaven where they saw "the greatest indifference to the concerns of eternity". In Aberdeen a very large crowd listened to Haldane's message outside the College on Romans 1.16, "I am not ashamed of the gospel of Christ for it is the power of God unto salvation to every one that believeth". Some may have been attracted by the novelty of the occasion, and to hear a former

East India Company Captain, but his powers as a preacher were becoming known.

The people of Banff were stirred to hear "Except ye repent, ye shall all likewise perish", and in Cullen tracts were distributed and the Gospel preached. In Elgin the magistrates forbade the bellman from intimating the preaching, yet at the appointed time around 600 people gathered in the street to hear a message proclaimed from the steps of the church. The journey continued through Forres and Nairn to Inverness where they learned that a fair was soon to take place in Kirkwall to which large numbers came from the outlying Orkney Islands. They sailed north to arrive on 12th August when they preached to above 800 persons gathered on open ground adjoining the cathedral church of St. Magnus.[5]

The next Lord's Day, Aikman preached to a congregation of 1,200, while Haldane crossed by boat to the island of Shapinsay, and preached standing on the shore. The visit was made memorable by the conversion of a man of ninety-two now confined to his bed. Haldane had gone to his cottage where the old man upon hearing of the Lord Jesus who had come to save, repeatedly exclaimed, "I believe, I believe". Midst all the excitement of preaching to large numbers in Kirkwall, Stromness and elsewhere, Haldane did not forget the old man, but revisited him before returning south via Caithness and Sutherland. This tour left solid results from conversions in many places, encouraged scattered believers, and led to the formation of *The Society for Propagating the Gospel at Home*.

To the South and West

A second extensive tour was undertaken in 1798 into Ayrshire, Galloway and the Borders. A Mr Watson, later a Congregational Church minister in Dumfries, was saved listening to Haldane preaching from John 3.3, while standing on the steps of the old cross of Ayr. Over 50 years afterwards he wrote, "In my imagination I see Mr James Haldane's manly form and commanding attitude, in youthful but dignified zeal, pouring out of the fulness of his soul a free, full, and everlasting salvation to the wondering multitude, who by the expression on their faces seemed to say 'we have heard strange things today' ".

Nettled by the impact of the lay preaching, the General Assembly of 1799 passed two declaratory acts "prohibiting all persons from preaching in any place under their jurisdiction who were not licensed", and forbidding "unauthorised teachers of Sabbath schools". This was aimed against men such as Haldane and Aikman who were contemptuously styled "vagrant teachers". These disgraceful measures were not rescinded until 1842.

The Northern Isles

Undeterred, Haldane decided to re-visit the north, and this time the tour extended to the Shetland Islands. On 10th July 1799 he arrived at Fair Isle where he preached the first sermon heard there for six years. He proceeded to Lerwick where he and his companion separated so they could cover a wider area. Haldane preached on the islands of Whalsay, Skerries, Fetlar, Yell and Unst as well as the remote Isle of Foula which then had 200 inhabitants and no resident minister. Years later Mr Haldane's son met a weather beaten seaman, who had piloted a Greenland whaler from Lerwick to Leith, who testified, "It was from your father I first heard the Gospel in Shetland over thirty years ago". After preaching at Sandwick in the south of Shetland they embarked on a six-oared open boat hoping to reach Fair Isle, 25 miles away, before dark. The ocean swell was heavy and they missed Fair Isle in the darkness, but Mr Haldane took the helm and steering by the stars headed for North Ronaldsay in Orkney. They passed it too, landing farther south on Sanday after a run of 54 miles. Travelling around these Northern Isles was no easy matter in those days!

Edinburgh Pastorate

James Haldane was pre-eminently an evangelist whose

itinerant ministry was singularly blessed of God in the awakening of many throughout Scotland. It was only after much deliberation that he accepted the invitation to be Pastor of the congregation in the Edinburgh Tabernacle Church. He and his brother sought to recover a form of church life more faithful to the New Testament, and the Tabernacles were formed as Congregational Churches. In 1808 James expressed his doubts as to the scriptural authority for infant baptism. Following a close study of the subject he was baptised.[6] He informed the Church that he regarded baptism as a matter for forbearance so that Baptist and Paedo-baptists might be in fellowship together, nevertheless a rupture followed as many could not accept their pastor's action and belief.

Pressing On

Local responsibility did not preclude itinerant preaching. Shorter tours were taken, for example along the Fife coast with a Mr Finlay, a native of Anstruther. At St Andrews, that ancient seat of learning, they found the town in spiritual darkness. No building was made available within which they could preach, so they went to the outskirts and Haldane stood on a millstone lying near the shore. At first few listened as Haldane read a psalm, but others came as Finlay raised the tune. Remembering the great events in the past Haldane announced his text, "When he beheld the city he wept over it". He warned the people to think of that Gospel which had been sealed with the blood of martyrs,[7] but was now supplanted by the preaching of a heartless and empty religious philosophy. His words impressed many, and next morning a multitude gathered while professors looked on with disdain, and the common people heard with gladness.

Over the years almost every town in Scotland heard the voice of James Haldane in fervent Gospel preaching. He enjoyed good health into old age and grasped every opportunity to preach Christ. On Lord's Day 2nd February 1851 he had expected to conclude an exposition of the Lord's farewell prayer but for the first time was unable to leave his house. On the Saturday of that week he entered into the joy of his Lord.

JB

Footnotes

1. Convoys were necessary to the protect the valuable ships and their cargoes from hostile French action.

2. The Socinian views of many of the Clergy was later countered by Robert Haldane's book *The Evidence and Authority of Divine Revelation.*

3. From *The Lives of Robert and James Haldane* published 1852, Banner of Truth 1990, pages 133/135

4. Ibid Ch. VI

5. Founded in 1137 by the Norse earl Rognvald who owed allegiance to the king of Norway

6. Robert Haldane was also baptised within a year of his brother.

7. This book, Chapters 5 and 6

CHAPTER 29

The Torch Today

Throughout this book we have been remembering some of the men and women who carried the torch of truth in previous centuries. We remember their work and their dedication, and the martyrdom of some, which have brought eternal benefits to millions throughout the world. We recall Hugh Latimer's words in 1555 as the fire began to burn while he was tied to Ridley at the stake, *"Play the man, Master Ridley; we shall this day light such a candle by God's grace in England, as I trust shall never be put out."* It has not been put out but burns brightly in every continent of the world. The torch passed on by others to others through those hundreds of years is now in our hands.

Into Our Hands

How privileged and honoured we are to be carrying the torch now, because being a torchbearer of the truth is more than reviewing the past. It was important through dark ages of ignorance and superstition, in times of fierce opposition from religious and secular powers, then during onslaughts of intellectualism, rationalism and higher criticism. But it is equally important now, in a new century of perhaps different types of opposition, be it more complicated intellectualism and rationalism, or secularism and materialism, militant atheism or agnosticism, political correctness and so-called 'equality', or just apathy and indifference to spiritual and eternal realities. We are called now to "shine as lights in the world", indeed we are privileged to do this. We can shine, yes we must - so that all those worthy characters who have gone before us will "not have run in vain, neither laboured in vain" as Paul exhorted (Phil 2.15-16).

Our cities, towns and villages are needy places, many of them as dark as night. From the leafy suburbs and the affluent neighbours to the dismal city centres with the poor, the homeless and destitute, from busy shopping malls and crowded sports arenas to lonely souls who never get a visit, from schools and colleges and universities to the ranks of the unemployed – each has its own problems and all need the Gospel. Can we take the torch within the reach of at least some of them? Our Lord's instructions are straightforward: "Let your light so shine before men" (Matt 4.16). Let it shine on everyone within our range, with good works as well as with clear words. Don't hide it under a bushel (of commerce?) or a bed (of indulgence?) (Mk 4.21).

Will we be mobilised to carry the torch somehow, just where we are? Every believer of every age group and of any ability can do it, so long as each is "a vessel, sanctified, and meet for the master's use" (2 Tim 2.21). Our Lord and Master's commission has not been withdrawn - to go and preach the gospel, to make disciples of all nations, to be His witnesses locally and to the uttermost parts of the earth, "into all the world," He said. (Mark 16.15; Matt 28.19; Acts 1.8).

"Into all the World"

The great age of missionary expansion from Great Britain (as it then was called), in the providence of God was facilitated by the infrastructure of the British Empire "on which the sun never set". In hazardous ocean voyages in sailing ships "driven of fierce winds", on board sturdier steamships on recognised trade routes, and then slowly thousands of miles on foot, on horseback, in oxcarts and in dugout canoes men and women went, their "feet shod with the preparation of the Gospel of peace".[1] They brought light to many who then sat in darkness and in the shadow of death. And now the torch of truth continues to burn in the hands of native believers who along with foreign missionaries light up the present darkness in every continent, in testimony to the Saviour of sinners.

But there are still many who have never heard, many held captive by hostile and harmful forces and by strong religious dogma. Will we attempt to reach them and rescue them? God still calls for willing servants to go, and thank God for the many who hear the call and are willing to go where He leads. His Word is also reaching into 'closed' societies by radio, satellite and internet channels, by digital means as well as by tried and tested literature routes. Let us pray that many will hear and believe as the torch blazes on.

Where it all Began

The torch of the Gospel was lit at Calvary, in dense darkness when the sun's rays were blotted out while our Saviour died alone, bearing the heavy load of our sins. Then He rose again and showed Himself alive to bring the message of great salvation, "which at the first began to be spoken by the Lord, and was confirmed unto us by those that heard Him" (Heb 2.3). Within a few years it had reached from Jerusalem into Judaea and Samaria (Acts 1.8), then into Europe and on to Rome the metropolis of a great empire from which it would radiate to "the uttermost part of the earth" (Acts 28).

That took place in the 1st century. But the great Gospel message does not need to be renewed for a different century, nor redesigned or its terms changed to suit a modern audience. Our duty is to pass it on as it is - for as it is, it is "the power of God unto salvation unto everyone that believes" (Rom 1.16). We have a stewardship of the truth received from the Lord Himself through those who have gone before us, for us to pass on to others coming after us, until "the end of the age" (Matt 28.20).

Sadly some have modified and obscured the light of the torch. Even early on some preachers invented "another gospel" (Gal 1.6-7). We know too that sometimes it has been preached from unworthy motives (Phil 1.15-16). But may none of these things distract us today from the honour of carrying unmodified this Gospel torch which was lit at Calvary. It is a "treasure in earthen vessels", fragile vessels of clay, so that the glory will be Christ's and not ours. Such vessels though fragile are required to contain the treasure, the torch inside which is "the light of the knowledge of the glory of God in the face of Jesus Christ" (2 Cor 4.6-7).

In these our present days of testimony and torchbearing let us make sure that we keep on shining this light out into the darkness all around us.

BC

Footnote

1. This is the subject of Volume 2 in this series, *Trailblazers and Triumphs of the Gospel.*

CHAPTER 30

"Lampstands" Today

Early on in the Book of Revelation we read of "golden lampstands" which the Lord had put in seven different places in Asia Minor long ago, churches which were testimonies to Him in a world of darkness, ignorance, sin and superstition. These churches were all different with different needs and difficulties, even different problems which required attention. Some were burning brightly, others much less so.

Each was autonomous, responsible to their Lord alone. None of them was asked to pass judgement on, or give opinions about the others. To them all He said, "I know thy works …" Of course these were not the only churches in that part of the world, just seven which were chosen to receive a particular message from the Lord.

Lamps in the Dark Ages

From then until now, believers in different parts of the world have gathered in such churches according to the Lord's command to remember Him in the "breaking of bread", and to proclaim the Gospel of His grace. But at times over the centuries these autonomous, scriptural churches ran into grave difficulties. The lamp burned dimly.

History tells us that the union of church and state led to formal organisations of churches which took over, and forcibly suppressed those which did not conform. Man-made religion and new superstitions spread through all of Christendom. The church grew rich and corrupt, the people poor and deprived of true spiritual guidance. Kept in ignorance of the Scriptures, the majority just accepted and submitted to the dogmas of the Church of Rome and its arrogant teachers, for not to do so was dangerous. It was conform or be cut off or even (and often) killed.

Yet the light was not extinguished, and as we have seen, a few educated individuals managed to obtain copies of at least part of the Greek New Testament. Convictions based on these scriptures led them to follow and practise apostolic teaching. Inevitably this resulted in head-on conflict with established religion which ruthlessly persecuted them, forcing them into hiding and secrecy. There they nevertheless obeyed the Word of the Lord, practising believers' baptism, weekly observance of the Lord's Supper, and preaching the Gospel of repentance and faith in Christ alone for salvation. Little has been left on record of these dear believers for obvious reasons, yet the stories of the Waldenses, the Moravian brethren, the Anabaptists and such like in central Europe make stirring and challenging reading.[1] The lamp may have been burning low, but the torch was still being carried onwards.

The Reformation and what followed

Earlier chapters of this book have surveyed the transforming Reformation movement in the 16th century. It was a significant break away from the Roman Church, asserting afresh the over-riding authority of the Scriptures now made more accessible, with renewed emphasis on faith not works for salvation. Men like Luther in Germany, Wycliffe and Tyndale in England, Knox in Scotland and all the brave martyrs who accompanied them, caused the great flame to burn more brightly again.

We have also noted how the torch was carried onwards through the 17th and 18th centuries by their successors, who boldly defended and proclaimed the truths recovered in the Reformation. Then in the early 19th century another significant development was the rediscovery of New Testament truths about local church practices, God's programme for the future, and the spread of the Gospel abroad. It looked as if the conditions described in the church at Philadelphia (Rev 3.7-13) arrived simultaneously in many parts of the British Isles, and in some places abroad.

Many local churches which function today according to the New Testament pattern trace their origins back to those days. During the 19th and early 20th centuries increasing numbers of these torches of truth were lit in countless cities, towns and villages throughout the UK and abroad. Many thousands of souls were saved, baptised, and then gathered into the name of the Lord Jesus alone in autonomous local churches, meeting in whatever types of buildings they could get or hire.[2]

Continuing Steadfastly

The hallmark of the early churches was that "they continued steadfastly in the apostles' doctrine and fellowship, and in breaking of bread, and in prayers" (Acts 2.42). Many assemblies of believers today still seek to do this. Their first and founder members saw it in the Scriptures, practised it, taught it, and passed it on. This torch of truth has now reached us. It is now in our hands, not as a 19th century tradition but as the doctrine of the Word of God which applies throughout all this age of grace.

Looking back over more than half a century, however, it is apparent that in the UK there have been great changes in assembly testimony. Some assemblies have changed so much it is difficult to recognise them. Some which were strong numerically and spiritually have become weak, and sadly some have ceased to exist. Reasons for this are not hard to find. Some reasons are understandable as employment patterns change and people move from one place to another. Also the advance of secularism and atheism has increasingly hindered the spread of the Gospel.

Other reasons are painful, as sadly we have to recognise that many divisions and subdivisions have weakened or even tragically destroyed assemblies. As a matter of history, major differences between sections of the professing church have centred on certain doctrinal matters which are not easily overlooked. But other divisions within some churches and assemblies have happened over trivial and personal matters, and should have been healed long ago. The record in this area even from early days is not good. It is painful to note how the devil has won victories, local testimonies have been weakened and many dear saints, young and old, have been distressed, disillusioned and lost the way because of it.

Challenging Times

Most of us now look back with great affection and respect to those who preceded us in the local churches where we now meet, and we thank God for their devotion, faithfulness and above all their example. We remember our guides, those who have spoken to us the Word of God (Heb 13.7). They showed us the way. Many of them brought us to where we are. Will we keep pressing on with the work they pioneered and established – not because it was their work or their idea, but the Lord's? Can we keep the torch burning?

Our times are quite different from theirs. Society is more apathetic. The tasks are many and our own numbers may be small. Our energies decrease as we get older. But God is the same and His Word is unchanged. The same Holy Spirit indwells us, enabling us for the tasks of today. The call to continue has not changed. Let's not think about giving up or closing down if at all possible! Let's keep the torch now in our hands burning brightly to pass on to the next generation until the Lord comes.

The devil is as active as ever "seeking whom he may devour". Influences from the world around are not conducive to distinctive assembly testimony, including the call of some interdenominational movements. Sadly they help the haemorrhage of valuable young people from the assemblies, and even some older ones too.

Let's make sure we teach especially our young people, why we do what we do. We must show a genuine interest in them, and involve them in the work of the assembly while setting them the clearest of examples of holiness and dedication to God.

More than ever we need to foster and develop local gift, and encourage its local use without relying so much and so often on "visiting speakers".

The command of the Lord is to preach the Word (2 Tim 4.2), to remember Him and show forth His death until He comes (1 Cor 11.26), to love one another with a pure heart fervently (1 Pet 1.22), to speak the truth in love, endeavouring to keep the unity of the Spirit in the bond of peace (Eph 4.3,15). The things which we ourselves have learned from faithful teachers of the Word we are to commit to faithful men who shall be able to teach others also (2 Tim 2.2).

Conclusion

Just as individual believers have been faithfully carrying the torch of the truth for a long time, so do assemblies of the Lord's people today in many places all over the world. In some places they are thriving with many people being reached and saved and added to their numbers, whilst in others they are struggling and finding that response to the gospel is meagre to say the least.

But let's not give up! Let us go on! (Heb 6.1).The Lord said, "That which ye have already, hold fast till I come!" (Rev 2.25).

Let us not fail in this great task. Let us keep the torch of testimony burning brightly!

BC

Footnotes

1. For example, *Miller's Church History* Vols 1, 2, & 3, Andrew Miller, 1925; *The Pilgrim Church*, E H Broadbent, 1931; both Pickering & Inglis

2. *Brethren, the Story of a Great Recovery*, D J Beattie 1940; reprinted 2011, John Ritchie Ltd.

APPENDIX

Timeline 1324 - 1837

1324 Birth of John Wycliffe

1348 The Black Death arrives in England. Over one third of the population died.

Circa 1440 Invention of the printing press in Germany by Johannes Gutenberg

1453 Fall of Constantinople and flight of Greek scholars to Italy

1454 Gutenberg Bible published. This Latin Vulgate version was the first book printed after the invention of moveable type.

1476 Caxton Printing Press begins in Westminster. William Caxton became the first retailer of books in England.

1509 – 1547 **Reign of Henry VIII**

1516 Publication by Erasmus of the first edition of his Greek New Testament

1517 Luther posts his 95 Theses to the door of All Saints Church Wittenberg

1526 Publication of Tyndale's complete New Testament in English

1547 – 1553 **Reign of Edward VI**

1553 – 1558 **Reign of Mary I** – English Martyrdoms

1558 – 1603	**Reign of Elizabeth I**
1603	Union of the Crowns - James VI of Scotland becomes James I of England.
1603 – 1625	**Reign of James I** (James VI of Scotland from 1567)
1620	The Pilgrim Fathers sail on board *Mayflower* to America.
1625 – 1649	**Reign of Charles I**
1642	Outbreak of English civil war
1643	Solemn League and Covenant adopted in Scotland.
1649	Execution of Charles I
1653 – 1658	Oliver Cromwell rules as Lord Protector.
1660	Restoration of the monarchy
1660 – 1685	**Reign of Charles II**
1680 – 1688	"Killing Times" for Scottish Covenanters
1685 – 1688	**Reign of James II** – the last Catholic monarch
1689 – 1702	**Reign of William III and Mary II** (daughter of James II) as joint monarchs (until Mary's death in 1694)
1689	The Glorious Revolution – ensured a Protestant succession to the throne.
1690	Battle of the Boyne
1692	The Glencoe Massacre
1702 – 1714	**Reign of Queen Anne** – sister to Mary II and the last Stuart monarch
1707	Act of Union – parliamentary union of Scotland with England

1714 – 1727	**Reign of George I**, first Hanoverian monarch of Great Britain
1727 – 1760	**Reign of George II**
1746	Battle of Culloden – last battle fought on British soil
1760 – 1820	**Reign of George III** – grandson of George II
1776	American Declaration of Independence
1789	Beginning of French Revolution
1805	Battle of Trafalgar and the death of Nelson
1815	Battle of Waterloo – Napoleon banished to St Helena
1820 – 1830	**Reign of George IV**
1830 – 1837	**Reign of William IV** – brother of George IV
1837	**Accession of Queen Victoria** – grand-daughter of George III

Torchbearers of the Truth

Torchbearers of the Truth